Dr Helen Street is an internationally acclaimed expert in wellbeing, education and applied social psychology, and a pioneer in long-term learning engagement and wellbeing through whole-school systemic change and development. An honorary fellow at The University of Western Australia, Helen has worked with more than 26,000 educators from more than 6000 schools and colleges in 16 countries, providing presentations, ongoing consultancy and support for increased Contextual Wellbeing. The Positive Schools Initiative, which she co-founded with Neil Porter, includes the highly respected Positive Schools conference series, and its pandemic-inspired Positive Schools Online, a global professional learning platform for educators passionate about supporting mental health. Helen is the author of four other books: Standing Without Shoes (with its foreword by His Holiness the Dalai Lama), Life Overload, Better than OK and Contextual Wellbeing, an international education best seller.

The Impossible question of living well

How do we hold on to what matters,
while also knowing how to let go?

Helen Street

Wise Solutions
Western Australia

WISE SOLUTIONS BOOKS

Published by Wise Solutions Pty Ltd
PO Box 634, Subiaco, WA 6904, Australia
+61 (0)8 93888843
enquiries@wisesolutions.com.au

First published by Wise Solutions 2024

Cover design by Troy Barbitta, Barbitta Creative + Design Studio
Photograph of Helen Street for TEDx Perth, used by permission
Inside design by Sonya Murphy

ISBN 978-0-9806397-9-7
ISBN (eBook) 978-0-9806397-0-4

For Neil
for standing in the center of the fire with me and never shrinking back

Endorsements

'A book imbued with huge amounts of wisdom and personal honesty? It's such a rare find, and for me made The Impossible Question of Living Well a richly worthwhile reading experience. I learned much from Helen Street's words.'

John Marsden, international best-selling author of the Tomorrow series and Ellie chronicles. Internationally acclaimed educator.

In life, everything changes. In this engaging book, Dr. Helen Street offers gems of wisdom on living with impermanence in all its forms: growth, change, loss, recovery, and growth again. Derived from her personal experiences, her Buddhist practice, and her scholarly work, these chapters go straight from the author's heart to the reader's, with gifts that are many and deep.

Professor Richard Ryan, Co-Founder of Self-Determination Theory. Professor - Institute for Positive Psychology and Education, Australian Catholic University, Sydney

"Helen has captured many of the elements of how to live a good life. Consider her your incredibly knowledgeable guide into using scientific insights to improve your own life."

Professor Todd B. Kashdan, author of 'The Upside of Your Dark Side' and 'The Art of Insubordination: How to Dissent and Defy Effectively'

If you are a human, this book is for you. The Impossible Question of Living Well challenges us to consider how the difficult times in our lives, despite their discomfort, are an essential part of living a whole life. Helen's candour and wisdom guides us on how we can learn to live with more ease, more acceptance, and greater connection. Intertwining wellbeing science with eastern philosophy, Helen's new book is one I will return to over and over again for its relevance to my personal and professional life. Thank you, Helen, for writing this book, for your honest stories of your life, for describing the lessons you've learnt along the way, and for sharing why both the highs and the lows in life are synonymous with the human experience.

Janis Coffey MAICD, Board Chair - Montessori Schools & Centres Australia (MSCA). Principal, North-Eastern Montessori School, Victoria, Australia

In this timely and thought-provoking book, Helen Street provides a personal and philosophical reflection on the pursuit of a balanced and meaningful life, acknowledging the inevitability of both positive and negative experiences. She emphasizes the importance of embracing the full spectrum of emotions and the transient nature of life. She delves into the challenges of navigating change, the power of negative emotions, and the concept of impermanence. She beautifully shares her own journey into Zen Buddhism and the integration of eastern philosophy with western social psychology to develop a synergic view of wellbeing. With her trademark sensitivity and compassion, Helen asks her readers to move away from the pursuit of a perpetually happy life and instead urges them to focus on deeply connecting to all aspects of life while accepting the constant nature of change. I loved it.

Dr Michael Carr-Gregg, child and adolescent psychologist, 'successful author, speaker, broadcaster and mental health advocate

This important and educative book presents a personal journey through numerous relational contexts where every changing and challenging life moment has been recognised, mined and acknowledged in a pivotal relational context with self, others and place. Helen has honestly portrayed her journey as a female, a partner, a mother, a social scientist and a teacher to lead others to a reality so crucial for wellbeing and for establishing meaning in life. We grow resilient relationally through better comprehending and appreciating life's contexts encountered. I find this book to be up with the best.

John Hendry OAM, educator and wellbeing advocate, acclaimed internationally for supporting relational approaches to wellbeing

Table of Contents

TABLE OF CONTENTS

The Invitation

By Oriah "Mountain Dreamer" House

"IT DOESN'T INTEREST ME what you do for a living. I want to know what you ache for, and if you dare to dream of meeting your heart's longing.

It doesn't interest me how old you are. I want to know if you will risk looking like a fool for love, for your dream, for the adventure of being alive.

It doesn't interest me what planets are squaring your moon. I want to know if you have touched the center of your own sorrow, if you have been opened by life's betrayals or have become shriveled and closed from fear of further pain. I want to know if you can sit with pain, mine or your own, without moving to hide it or fade it or fix it.

I want to know if you can be with joy, mine or your own, if you can dance with wildness and let the ecstasy fill you to the tips of your fingers and toes without cautioning us to be careful, to be realistic, to remember the limitations of being human.

It doesn't interest me if the story you are telling me is true. I want to know if you can disappoint another to be true to yourself; if you can bear the accusation of betrayal and not betray your own soul; if you can be faithless and therefore trustworthy.

I want to know if you can see Beauty, even when it's not pretty, everyday, and if you can source your own life from its presence.

I want to know if you can live with failure, yours and mine, and still stand on the edge of the lake and shout to the silver of the full moon, "Yes!"

It doesn't interest me to know where you live or how much money you have. I want to know if you can get up, after the night of grief and despair, weary and bruised to the bone and do what needs to be done to feed the children.

It doesn't interest me who you know or how you came to be here. I want to know if you will stand in the center of the fire with me and not shrink back.

It doesn't interest me where or what or with whom you have studied. I want to know what sustains you, from the inside, when all else falls away.

I want to know if you can be alone with yourself and if you truly like the company you keep in the empty moments."

By Oriah "Mountain Dreamer" House from her book,
THE INVITATION © 1999. Published by HarperONE,
San Francisco. All rights reserved.
Presented with permission of the author. www.oriah.org

INTRODUCTION

IF YOU ARE SUSPICIOUS of 'happy ever after' endings, and consider the pursuit of a cheery life to be an impossible 'catch 22', then this is the book for you. Absolutely you want to experience an abundance of happy times, but you also want to feel justified and confident when embracing sadness, grief, anger and the whole universe of other 'negative' emotions that arise when life is tough. Indeed, you know that no matter who you are, or what you do, life is sometimes tough; and tough times demand tough emotions, thoughts and feelings. You know it is important to ask how we might better embrace both the light and dark sides of living and being, rather than how we might find light in everything. As such, you are putting your hand up for the idea of living a passionate and connected life, rather than the futile pursuit of one that is devoid of pain.

All Things are Temporary

No matter how good a time, a relationship or an experience might be, it can only ever be temporary. Even the most deeply cemented relationships and the most authentic connections, will eventually end, even if only due to our own demise. This means that, in order to live life as fully as we can, we need to know how to connect deeply, meaningfully and whole-heartedly to all the good times in our lives, while also being able to navigate the pain of tough times and loss.

This challenge can seem like an impossible question. But if we can address it successfully, we not only strengthen our ability to accept change, we gain the freedom to live life to the full.

I have been a social psychologist for more than 30 years. This means I have long been interested in how our connection to the world impacts us as individuals and as social beings. More specifically, I have been keen to understand how the social contexts of our lives influence our view of both ourselves and the world around us; and consequently, guide our capacity for both wellbeing and resilience. Learning to deal with the ups and downs of life takes practice, along with the development of self-awareness and self-belief. It also takes accepting the inevitability of change, including the constantly changing nature of our social identity within a constantly changing world. I have written this book to help all of us embrace change and find relief in knowing that life does not always have to go well to be well.

My professional interest in the social side of wellbeing was ignited by a personal desire to improve my own wellbeing, and to manage adversity more effectively. I have long sought to find a philosophy that is not merely coherent and rational but resonates deeply with me and helps me feel more alive. I could never quite trust messages prioritising the pursuit of happiness or understanding resilience as being able to meet pain with happy emotions. They always seemed to be selling me an impossible dream of an artificial, permanent state of being. Encouraging me to believe that, if I could find some sort of consistent fixed smile, all would be well. Even if this had been possible, I am not sure I could ever feel totally alive in such a one-sided world; nor would I be able to live fully. As much as we may seek constancy, I believe that we know at some deep level that we really need change.

I found the beginnings of my awakening in the words and ideas of twentieth century philosophers. In particular, Alan Watts, DT Suzuki and Joseph Campbell; all of whom drew heavily on Zen Buddhist teachings to inform their work and ideas. Buddhism is most easily understood as a mix of religion and philosophy. It developed from the teachings of an Indian spiritual teacher called Gotama around the 5th centuries BC. Since its Indian beginnings, Buddhim spread from India to Central and Southeast Asia, China, Korea, and Japan, and finally to the Western World in the early twentieth century.

Zen Buddhism is a branch of Buddhism that is best known for its consideration of enlightenment (known as satori). Enlightenment has many magical connotations associated with it, but is most simply understood as a profound awareness and understanding of life. Zen Buddihists believe that enlightenment is attainable by anyone who invests in enough studying, contemplating and meditating on Buddhist teachings. The possibility of becoming 'spontaneously enlightened' was an undeniably attractive proposition to many impatient young westerners. As such, Zen Buddhism became popular among many young people seeking an early form of self-help in the 1960s and 1970s. The profound impact of both Watt's and Campbell's work on my life, and my own search for life's meaning, led to me taking my own journey into Zen and Buddhism. My interest in Zen Buddhism was therefore, not so much as a religious pursuit, but to learn to live more fully, with more passion, meaning and purpose.

Now, having spent more than 25 years combining my understanding of western social psychology with my understanding of traditionally eastern philosophy, I have created my own synergic view of the science and art of wellbeing. One that is grounded in scientific research and understanding, but also resonates with me personally. It is a view which acknowledges the complexities of living well, along with the complexities of dealing with trauma and challenge. As such, it is also a view that requires consideration, application and a desire to play the long game of fierce living.

On my journey I have written many academic papers, general articles, book chapters and several books, but none as personal or as vulnerable as this. As such, this book feels particularly special and significant to me. It offers a very personal sharing of my philosophical understanding of the world. I hope it will resonate and offer value to you.

The Power of Negative Emotions

I fear that our desire to be positive, and to seek positivity in all we do, has in fact, led to us pathologising appropriate negative feelings and emotions. Rather than asking ourselves how our identity has been challenged when we feel sad or anxious, we have been encouraged to probe what is 'wrong' with us and how we can 'feel better'. Similarly, we have been encouraged to 'cheer up' when we are sad, often with little consideration of the actual value of feeling unhappy. For sure, negative emotions can be hard to bear, sometimes get out of hand, and can leave us longing for respite. Yet, when expressed mindfully and appropriately, they serve an important purpose, and offer us direction. As such, they are worthy of as much acceptance as their positive counterparts. Distress, however hard, helps us to identify a fracture within ourselves. It demands our time out from the world, our introspection and our attention. Appropriate negative emotions help us to be resilient when we need to be. They guide us to examine and re-discover ourselves when we feel fractured or threatened, so that we might repair ourselves in an authentic and workable way.

The Impermanence of Life

The reality of life is that it ends. Even if we believe in a spiritual after-life, or in re-birth, the life that we know now will ultimately, inevitably be gone. If we spend all our time trying to find the joy in life, the consistency in ourselves, and the beauty in the moment without acknowledging this fact, our wellbeing can only ever be superficial. Death is indeed distressing and scary, and not necessarily something we want to dwell on, especially when everything in our life is going well.

The reality of death will, however, always be present and known in the back of our minds. Unless we can consciously accept its reality, it will hold us in fear, diminishing even the most joyous of moments. As such, an acknowledgement and acceptance of the impermanence of life helps us to embrace all of life more fully.

Thus, I believe a large missing piece of the modern mental health jigsaw is an understanding and accepting of the reality of 'impermanence'. If we do not openly live with an acceptance of change, we find ourselves seeking consistency as a mirage of wellbeing, and can end up keeping our sun-seeking head in the sand.

Connection, Context and Change

> *'The only way to make sense out of change is to plunge into it, move with it, and join the dance.'* Alan Watts

'Connection' is a word we hear a lot nowadays; however our ideas of connection are often limited and even diminished due to our inability to accept the inevitability of change. In fact, we often measure the success of a connection with time: for example, celebrating our relationships in years served, rather than in their meaning and depth. This is arguably because of our determined search for a 'happy ever after', and our relentless setting of goals that we believe will help us achieve the elusive outcome of 'forever happiness'. It is ironically as if we believe a pathway of change will lead to some sort of final 'happy' consistent end.

Change is not something we can avoid or turn on and off. For sure, some things change faster than others – young children seem to change day to day, whereas older relatives seem far more constant – but change always continues. As such, being deeply and meaningfully connected to someone or something does not mean being permanently connected and hanging on for dear life. Rather, meaningful connection is about becoming a part of a unique moment in time, knowing it can never last and will never be repeated. It is worth being reminded that the Buddhist concept of 'non-attachment' is not about avoiding attachment but rather, is about learning to connect deeply while also understanding the impermanence of life.

This book is for anyone who wants to address the impossible question of living well; to know how to connect deeply to all aspects of life, while also knowing that everything changes, always. The search for a perpetually sunny life, or for the utopia of our dreams, is not only impossible, it is not enough. As we learn to embrace the ongoing creation of our lives, may we learn to hold onto an authentic understanding of ourselves, nurturing acceptance and building our resilience, while all the time, everything changes.

ONE

When it Matters, it Matters

UNWANTED ADVERSITY AND LOSS come in many guises, impacting us in many ways. Be it the resentment that grows from losing a job, the pain of a relationship break up or the unimaginable weight of losing someone we love dearly. You may have experienced the disenfranchised grief that kept so many people languishing during the peak of the COVID pandemic, or the loss of identity that accompanies a big life change such as moving overseas to live. You may have gone through an acrimonious divorce; lost a best friend, partner or parent; failed your exams or had to deal with the burden of chronic illness.

Alternatively, you may find yourself dissatisfied, disengaged or disconnected...without really knowing why.

Adversity and loss take on many forms, and our reaction to it varies in terms of impact, intensity and 'bear-ability'. Yet, no matter what or how much we struggle, we tend to find ourselves asking similar questions. Questions such as: 'When will I feel better?', 'How can I get over this?', 'Can I make sure this never happens again?', 'Will I ever stop thinking, crying, talking about feeling bad?', 'How can I heal?', 'Will I ever move on?'

Losing Simon

My first memorable experience of loss was relatively small and simple as a significant life event, but it meant the world to me at the time.

It involved the death of our family dog, Simon, when I was seven years old. It was not a loss I would compare to tougher times I have experienced as an adult. Still, as a young child, it was a loss that fractured me to the core. After all, when it matters, it matters.

Simon had come from the dog rescue home to join our family as an unwanted young adult. He was part beagle, always in search of food, and a bit overweight. Although initially very nervous of him, I quickly came to consider this gentle, happy creature to be my absolute best friend. He followed me everywhere, which I took as a sign of complete devotion. Looking back, it was probably more because I was always dropping crackers, crisps and other bits of tempting food.

When my beautiful dog died, I found it hard to understand the finality of the situation. I had loved Simon so very deeply and could barely remember who I was before he had been around.

On the day of Simon's death, my parents broke the news gently but honestly. Looking back as an adult, I am grateful they didn't pretend he had gone to some canine version of Disneyland, and I was given the chance to realise and accept that pets die. Still, at the time I was very angry indeed. I sobbed uncontrollably for hours, beside myself with emotion, struggling to appreciate that this was something no one could fix. It seemed awful, insurmountable and completely unfair.

The only solution seemed to be to leave home immediately. So, after an afternoon of weeping, I packed my small pink suitcase with my favourite toys and promptly proceeded out the door. I made it as far as the gate before my mother gently walked me back inside. She hugged me for the entire evening.

A very short time later, perhaps the next day, my dad and I sat down with a book about different breeds of dog. Its pages were glossy and inviting and, despite my initial reluctance to look through it, I was soon deeply committed to getting a glamorous dalmatian or perhaps an exotic red setter.

A few weeks later we adopted Judy, a Labrador cross, also a rescue animal. The moment I met her, I fell in love.

Simon's death was a painful and difficult experience for a young me to navigate, but also an opportunity to learn a little about the inevitability of loss and grief, and what it means to be resilient. I began to understand the importance of honouring our emotional experience to loss; and how to accept the reality that unwanted things happen to all of us.

My identity was tied up with my beloved pet and, as such, had been fractured by his death. I had, however, benefitted from the reassurance of other important connections that defined me in the world, namely my sympathetic parents. Once I began to consider my world without my beloved Simon, I started to repair myself with the hope that grows when we begin to believe that things will be alright once more, even if different. Finally, I began to redefine myself. This, for me, meant developing the courage to invest in another meaningful relationship with a new pet, clear in the knowledge that it, too, would one day be gone.

Since that childhood experience of grief, many other failures, deaths and broken relationships have come and gone in my life, as they do for us all. I have navigated the deep sadness of losing friends and family, a derailing of my sense of self due to lost friendships, and the rollercoaster pain of divorce. I have also, like so many others, had to deal with lost job opportunities, lost goals and a realisation that even the most precious things in life are temporary.

The Pain of Loss and Longing

Three other immense experiences stick significantly in my mind, largely because each also provided a new experience of loss, and therefore changed my worldview profoundly. The first was when I was a teenager, and the suicide of a close friend left me numb and untrusting of the fragility of life. I vividly remember my friend giving me a lift home from the pub. We listened to his favourite songs as we drove, playing loudly from his tape deck. I knew all the words to Mungo Jerry's 'In the Summertime' and sang it badly, at full volume. It was fun, and everything seemed fine between us. But as we pulled into my family driveway, my friend, out of the blue, told me he wanted to kill himself. His shocking words seemed to punch at the air and then just hang there, in the silence that immediately followed. In that entirely unexpected moment, I gingerly, inadequately, tried to broach the enormous existential question: Why? He didn't want to tell me.

In some awful twist of fate, I had experienced a significant assault that very same day. I was consequently disengaged, upset and tired, having spent hours in a police station filing a report. My friend's call for help now seemed totally surreal and completely overwhelming. I remember him insisting we play an awful game of me trying to guess what was wrong. I tried to encourage him to tell me, while also feeling numb with the weight of my own distress. I tried to advise him to talk to someone, anyone. To me, to a doctor, to someone who might be able to help...

My friend died the very next day. He used the shotgun he had kept in his car, a part of his farming life. He had just turned twenty-one.

It was the beginning of my unravelling as a teenager, although it could well be said that the threads had been loosening for a long time. I remember feeling paralysed when I heard the news. It had seemed absolutely unreal. My parents suggested I would be fine as 'young people are resilient'. We never discussed what had happened or how I was coping. They had hoped I might choose to approach them and talk about it if ever I wanted. I didn't.

Around the World in 26 Hours

A completely different experience of loss occurred years later when I emigrated to Australia at age 32. It was then that, despite being excited to move to the 'sunny country' on the other side of the world and embrace all its unknowns, I found myself painfully homesick, aching for all I had left behind. My parents, my friends, my support networks.

I became engulfed in a disenfranchised grief that took me by surprise; and which was hard to pin down and unpack. I can't say that I was distraught – I was embarking on a thrilling adventure, after all – but I definitely languished badly. Absolutely I missed my English family and friends deeply, but this I had expected. What I had not anticipated was the enormous longing I felt for the smallest of details of my everyday English life. I carried around a yearning for Boots the chemist, the BBC evening news and an opportunity to go to the pub for last orders.

It was the first time in my life that I really understood how much our identities are entwined with all that we are connected to in the contexts of our lives. Not just the people, but the culture, the physical environment and all the little things that make life, make sense.

Dad

Third, and the toughest of all, was the loss of my father when I was 49. When he reached the age of eighty, I knew the end of Dad's life was starting to come into view. I hoped he would live for many more years, but he had experienced a long-term struggle with heart disease and other serious health concerns. I found myself frequently wondering how I would react when he died. It was as if I were trying to prepare myself for the inevitability of my future distress. As if I could somehow 'practise grief'.

When the dreaded time came for real, my older brother Ken woke me with an early morning call and told me our father had died of a heart attack a few hours ago. Suddenly, there was no turning back. I felt immediately frozen in an indelible moment, but also completely distraught.

My mother had called Ken to let him know straight away, and he had driven the two-and-a-half-hour trip to be with her... in well under two hours. I remember thinking: 'I am so glad you arrived safely before I knew you had to make the drive.'

The situation was enormous. Yet, all the time I was reacting, acting in the midst of this acute painful moment in 2015, a moment to which I was instantly so indelibly connected, I also had a totally disconnected part of me staying calm and aware. This central part of my identity, this inner voice, noticed that I had not reacted in any of the ways I had 'rehearsed' in my imagination.

I remember briefly thinking: 'Oh. So, this is what it is really like. This is how I really feel, and this is my real reaction. Not quite as rehearsed or imagined. Less dramatic in fact...but, oh, so much more deeply painful.' I also remember realising that, as much as I was drowning in the moment, that deep voice in me was standing on the shore with a hand outstretched to keep me holding on.

My social self had been shattered in one major blow but my inner voice kept it together enough for the whole of me to function, and eventually repair. Connection and reconnection are everything, and they start deep within ourselves.

Six months after my father died, I found myself repeatedly in tears as I attempted to work. Sometimes triggered by a song on the radio, sometimes a smell of rain in the air, sometimes the sight of his picture, or simply a passing thought. On one of these occasions, I apologised to my partner Neil for being so upset...yet again. Neil looked at me struggling to contain my tears and said: 'Grief is a process. You have to go through it to get over it. It's as simple as that.' He was right. Unless you can go through it, you can't get over it. And that takes time.

Around the same time, a close friend – who had also lost a much-loved parent – told me that it had helped her pain to understand grief as an extension of love. How true this is. The more we are connected and defined by our relationship with someone or something, the more we grieve when we lose it. When it matters, it matters.

For me, my relationship with my father was incredibly significant and so it was unsurprising that it took me many months to heal. Similarly, the despondency I felt when I moved to Australia reflected the love I have for a country where I had spent the first thirty-two years of my life. Consequently, it would be easy to contemplate that the 'cure' to grief is the avoidance of 'too much' love and of being too deeply attached. This is certainly a strategy used by some. Yet, losing the opportunity of love is akin to losing the opportunity to experience belonging, connection and the feeling of being truly alive. And that is no way to live well.

So rather than avoid connection, how can we find a way to connect to our lives but also accept and recover from the painful experiences of loss? How can we move on from loss without regret or resentment? How can we move forward with the courage to make new, deep connections, defining ourselves according to things that matter, but do not last?

Ultimately, is it possible to love deeply, and to also know how to let go?

How to hold onto yourself when the world lets go

In the following chapters you will find a mix of modern western psychology, ancient eastern wisdom and personal reflection. We begin with a discussion of identity, personality and the creation of each of us as a 'me' in a social world. We'll then look to the social contexts that make us and ask not simply 'How can we be improved?' but also, 'How can we meet our most important needs within the contexts of our lives?'

We examine impermanence and learn that the essence of living well is knowing, really knowing, that everything changes, always. With our understanding of impermanence at hand, we then consider the nature of progress and re-visit our goals as signposts to our values.

Finally, we look to understand that, throughout the highs and lows of our ever-changing existence, there is always room for hope. Not a hope that is blind to the realities of an ever-changing impermanent life, but a hope that knows everything really will be alright...mostly.

Ultimately, I hope this book helps you to understand the impact of the adversity and losses you face in your life – and to heal. I also hope it helps you have the courage to feel truly alive in this complex, beautiful and temporary world.

TWO

Holding On and Letting Go

NOT ONLY DOES ADVERSITY and loss come in many guises, it comes to us all. No matter how hard we try to avoid the pain of tough times, it catches us many times over. From the frustrations of missed opportunities, to the deepest cries of grief, we are all impacted. We all struggle. We all sometimes believe life is unfair, even unbearable. And this is undeniably hard.

It is no wonder that the self-help market has invested so much time, energy and money in exploring how we might become emotionally 'safer', spend more time feeling 'happier' and ultimately avoid the pain of loss at all. And then, when all this fails, that same self-help market asks how we might recover more quickly, and less painfully, when tough times occur. Certainly, the concept of resilience has become big business in recent times.

But, perhaps the pain of hard times is *not* something it is good to escape from, at least not completely. In fact, perhaps it is possible to make the pain of losing something or someone more bearable, more acceptable. Perhaps there is a better way to understand and be at peace with our tough times. A way that is more supportive of our future well-being. A way that will, ultimately, help us move on with a sense of hope and possibility.

Adversity and loss are unavoidable in a life well lived, however, we would not find a better life if we could avoid them. Even though at times loss is undeniably hard. As such, it is imperative we do not think of resilience as the ability to create an emotional coat of armour, keeping us protected from the pain of loss, for that may well be the greatest loss of all. It is also vital we do not mistake the avoidance of loss with success; if anything, avoiding all loss is arguably the greatest failure of all. Rather, resilience is more about honouring, accepting and healing from the pain of adversity than it is about avoiding it all together. It is more about connecting with passion than it is about avoiding the risk of connection for fear of experiencing pain. It is more about connecting deeply than about being detached, however tough or risky this might appear to be.

A Life for all Seasons

We can more readily embrace the good times, and more easily accept the tough times, when we think of our life as a constantly turning spiral of identity creation, fracture and repair. Wellbeing and resilience are both integral parts of this spiral.

Consider the spiralling pathway continually turning through the ever-changing seasons of life. As is the way with many new births, we are born at the beginning of our very own spring. From our first breath of spring air, our identity formation begins. First, as an individual human being and then as a socially constructed person.

When our early life is nurturing and healthy, we enjoy an increasing sense of belonging and engagement in the world. This gives us an increasing sense of our wholeness, so that we feel happy and full of life. As we grow, we navigate through spring showers, developing and learning as we head into the warmth of the summer sun. It is at this time that we experience life with the most contentment, commitment and joy.

Despite our best efforts to hold on to the moment, our happy experience of summer, just like all experiences, will eventually pass. This happens when something tough inevitably happens and our wellbeing is challenged. As such, finding fulfilment does not mean we have found a permanent happily ever after. Eventually the autumn rain will arrive: something significant will go wrong. Adversity and loss will always come knocking, and we will face unwanted struggle and pain. We may lose an important friendship, a grandparent or a loved pet. We may lose a race we were heavily invested in, be it for academic achievement, sport or parental favour. When these things happen to us, we no longer feel so whole or so well. Our identity moves into the inevitable chill of winter. We feel fractured, broken or lost and this means, to a greater or lesser degree, we struggle and we suffer.

As time passes, however, when we are resilient, winter also comes to an inevitable end. We learn to honour and accept our wounds, and we look beyond our loss, to repair and to heal. We then continue our journey into a new spring, in search of a renewed sense of ourselves and our place in the world. We re-emerge with a new way for everything to be OK.

We travel around this spiral of identity creation, fracture and recreation many times over in life. Such is the continuing passing of the seasons of our identity, until we face the greatest, most final loss of all: the loss of ourselves completely.

This constant spiral of identity creation, fracture and recreation is a way of understanding both our wellbeing and our need for resilience as interdependent and inevitable. In particular, it helps us to understand resilience as something that is only possible when we accept the ever-changing cyclical nature of our existence as a unique person in a socially constructed world.

No matter how whole and happy our life seems, we will always, eventually, need to face the inevitability of adversity and loss. Once we can do this genuinely, even if unwillingly, we can better embrace the art of reconnection, recovery and the return of hope.

Our understanding of this spiralling cycle reminds us that each aspect of our socially created self is born from connections made in an

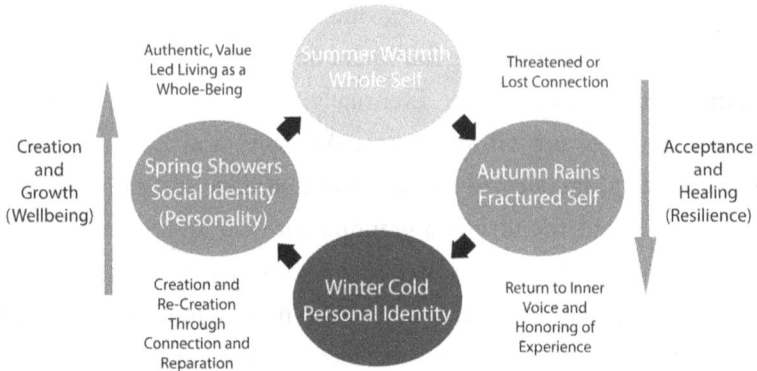

The Ever Changing Creation and Recreation of Self
© Dr Helen Street

impermanent world. It helps us to realise that resilience is about creating and recreating our identity, not about preserving it. It helps us to find the courage to connect and reconnect, rather than avoid meaningful connections and the risk of loss. The cycle shows us that the connections we need to feel whole will eventually be lost, but we can always find a way to move on and feel whole again, albeit in a different way than before. This cycle continues until finally we meet the ultimate loss and face our own end. As such, the cycle of our identity creation and recreation is an admission of our own impermanence, as much as it is a representation of the impermanence of our socially created world.

Celebrating Our Continual Creation

This consideration of the changing inevitability of life is, however, nothing to be sad or anxious about. It is indeed an acknowledgement of the fragility and challenge of life. But in this, it is also a constant reminder of the creative, restorative and joyous aspects of connection and the creation of ourselves as a person. Ultimately, understanding this unstoppable cycle of our identity helps us to appreciate that the beauty of life lies in its dynamic and temporary nature. The more we can understand this, the more we can embrace all that is incredible in every fleeting sunny moment, and the more we can be resilient when it rains. Simply put, understanding our constantly turning cycle of identity means we are better equipped to treasure the good times and better able to heal when times get tough.

So how does all of this philosophising over the nature of identity creation and recreation help us in practical, tangible terms? How can we move from a theoretical understanding to a lived experience?

In addressing these important questions, I hope to offer ideas, suggestions and discussion that will resonate with you and help you to experience greater wellbeing during the good times, and be more resilient when life gets tough.

Be warned. I am not offering a five-step plan, or even a ten-step one. I am not providing a quick fix to feeling better about things going wrong. Rather, I invite you to join me on a journey of exploration and discussion about the nature of identity and how we might meaningfully, authentically embrace our ever-changing existence, with courage, clarity and confidence.

THREE

Creating a Foundation for Resilience

UNDERSTANDING THE CYCLICAL, SEASONAL nature of our social identity creation and re-creation helps us to realise that, when we lose someone or something that matters, we suffer. Yet, we do not suffer because that something or someone has gone. Rather, we suffer because losing something or someone means we lose the part of ourselves that was defined by our relationship with that which has gone. As such, loss changes our experience of the world because it challenges our social identity, 'who we are as a person'. The more we define ourselves by a relationship, the more our identity is threatened or fractured when that relationship is broken or lost.

If we try to live a disengaged life, or to protect our fragile selves from threat or damage, we lose the opportunity to become our best selves, and to live well. For it is only through the cycle of connection and reconnection that we become whole and can be wholly reconnected within the world.

So, the question remains, how do we love deeply – and also learn to let go?

Finding the Balance

To begin, it helps to understand that loss and grief are not only inevitable, they are essential elements of a life lived to the full. We need to realise that if we pursue a life lived 'happily ever after' we are sure going to be disappointed many times over. A search for some 'safe' world – in which loss never happens and we never experience grief is not just futile, it is a search for loneliness and despondency. A meaningful life is filled with a mix of the good and the great, along with the mediocre and the bad, and sometimes the terrible. Feeling cheerful all the time is simply not an option, at least not without a lot of self-medication and denial.

Yet, in recent times, it seems we have been led to believe that happiness is the ultimate measure of success – indeed, the existence of the annual World Happiness Report suggests that entire countries can be judged and ranked on the happiness of their people – and that feelings of sadness, loss and grief represent failure and fear. A bit like living in a varied climate, but only venturing outside in the summer.

What's more, we have been encouraged to equate being happy with having lots of stuff, lots of status and lots of money. We have come to believe that we will be more protected from distressing, unhappy feelings if only we can become richer, more adulated, more comfortable. It is not surprising that we often set our sights on attaining the things that we believe will provide protection from distress, be they based in the material world or in the judgements of others. It is understandable that so many of us aim to have more wealth, more status, more recognition, greater popularity and certainly more possessions. We have been consistently persuaded, without much questioning, that having 'more' external things equates to feeling 'more' internally positive about everything we have more of...and helps us avoid unwanted feelings of sadness and loss. Unfortunately, this belief system is diminishing our capacity for resilience, rather than increasing it, and leading to more suffering rather than less.

For the Love of Money

The relationship between money and wellbeing is a complex one. I am not suggesting that money cannot buy any level of contentment at all. Rather, wellbeing studies like one conducted by researchers David Blanchflower and Andrew Oswald in 2004, and another by Christopher Boyce in 2010, have shown that, at least in the more materially driven parts of the world, wealthy people are generally happier than those who have less money. This is not, however, because wealthy people are jubilantly enjoying daily champagne, nice though I am sure that would be. It is because they are more likely to experience high levels of respect and status within their communities, while also avoiding the stress and pressure of trying to keep up with their neighbours. Thus, it is the impact of being connected and respected within our communities that mediates the impact of money on wellbeing.

In contrast, many people who are struggling financially while living in materially-driven parts of the world face a great deal of trauma. Not only must they deal with the challenges of maintaining their basic living requirements such as food, shelter and health care, they also have to live with the knowledge that they are somehow considered to be at the bottom of their community's scale of success. They have the stress and overwhelm of tough living and the loneliness of low status and a lack of community belonging. In parts of the world that are less materially-driven, materially poor people often still achieve high levels of wellbeing and a strong sense of belonging. This is not to say that life is not challenging for them, or often traumatic and far too short. But rather to acknowledge that the relationship between wealth and wellbeing is mediated by belonging and status more than our beliefs about what money can buy. Beyond a basic need for survival, wellbeing is not about having wealth per se.

In 2003 I published my first book *Standing Without Shoes*, which focused on the idea that we would all be less vulnerable to depression if only we understood happiness and wellbeing more fully. I wrote the book with friend and colleague George Burns, and the Dalai Lama generously wrote the foreword. During this time, George asked the Dalai Lama why the working-class people of Bhutan, a country in which His Holiness frequently travelled, seemed so much happier than middle-class people in the US. George was curious to know why people with seemingly so little were so much happier than those who seemed to have so much. Many of the Bhutanese people he had met had minimal income, very basic accommodation and food, and barely any health care at all. In contrast, the middle-class Americans who George had met during his US travels seemed to have an abundance of stuff. They boasted multiple cars and computers, and TVs in every room of their homes, and most of them ate out every week. Yet, they seemed so much more stressed and discontented than the poor people in Bhutan.

The Dalai Lama was quick to suggest that the Bhutanese people George knew did not consider themselves to have less than their American counterparts. In fact, it was quite the opposite – they felt they had more of the things by which they defined themselves and their success. Unlike the Americans, the Bhutanese people were more likely to measure success in terms of their family bonds, friendships and their own spiritual journey to knowing themselves. They embraced all aspects of life with a feeling of abundance.

Things become more complicated when we consider unexpected financial gains. A lot of early prominent research suggested that, even in the materially-driven developed world, we are no happier following, say, large lottery wins. Most notably a highly referenced study by Philip Brickman and his colleagues in 1978 suggested that lottery winners were no happier a year after their windfall than they had been before it. Brickman's findings led to many psychologists and 'wellbeing experts' confidently stating that 'money does not buy happiness' at all. More recent research suggests that, maybe it does make a difference, at least if the win is moderate. For example, research by Jonathan Gardner and Andrew Oswald in 2007 suggests that medium-sized wins have no immediate impact on wellbeing but can make a difference to longer-term happiness two years later. (Medium-sized meaning that the amount is within reach of our peers who work hard and save well). So, it seems that unexpected, moderate financial gains help us to garner the status and acceptance we crave, without the associated pressure and stress of working hard to maintain that financial status. These gains have a similar impact to being relatively wealthy: they help us to feel accepted as valuable members of our communities.

Having more stuff, does not, in itself, equate to feeling more whole and having more long-term wellbeing. But it is undeniable that material wealth can provide us with opportunities to embed ourselves more deeply *into* community life. If we are considered ridiculously rich, however, the relationship between wealth and wellbeing changes again. When very wealthy, we are likely to be elevated all the way *out* of our communities because we are no longer seen as being equivalent to our neighbours. I wonder how many very wealthy or renowned people complain of feeling isolated or excluded from the people they have worked so hard to impress?

For most of us, lottery wins and other desirable financial gains such as an inheritance are not a regular or even a one-time occurrence. Moreover, even if we do attain material comfort, community acceptance is not always guaranteed, and we will certainly still experience unwanted losses. We all face loss, tragedy and unforeseen trauma, regardless of financial status. We all face suffering, rejection and a fractured sense of ourselves in some capacity to a greater or lesser degree.

So, if having 'more' status and stuff is hard to attain, no guarantee of long-term wellbeing and no safeguard against loss, what can we do to build and rebuild our wellbeing through the highs and lows of life?

How can we learn the art of resilience?

Resilience and the Importance of Meaningful Connections

Simply put, the answers to these questions lie in our ability to know our innermost self, to find belonging within our social contexts—for instance, our work communities, our families, our friend groups – and to understand that everything changes, always. We live our best life when we see, hear and respect our inner voice and when we learn to make healthy connections, both within ourselves and externally in the ever-changing social contexts of our lives.

When we develop healthy connections within our social contexts, we experience a greater sense of belonging, meaning and purpose. This means we have a greater sense of wellbeing. The more wellbeing we have, the more we are likely to demonstrate resilience when we lose something important, whether we are materially rich or poor. When we have healthy connections, we experience a strong sense of ourselves and our place in the world, even when things are not going our way.

The art of resilience is about learning to heal when times are tough and reflects our ability to live well when times are good. It begins with self-awareness and self-acceptance. It also includes the ongoing development of authentic social connections that meet our core needs for belonging, engagement and voice. We need to make these social connections with the people around us, the spaces we make into places, the norms that reflect our values, and the things that we do. Our day-to-day wellbeing is therefore stronger when we connect to family and friends with authentic relationships, find flow in our actions, and create meaning in the space we call home.

Healthy connections help us to feel valued and valuable even when life is fragmented or relationships are broken. When we are meaningfully connected within ourselves and within our social contexts, we have the capacity to hold ourselves and to live our life to the full no matter what struggles we are experiencing.

When Connections Make Healing Harder

Avoiding authentic connections does nothing to protect us from experiencing the pain of loss. If we form connections that are superficial or lack meaning, we still tend to grieve when they are broken. For example, we may still feel rejected by the loss of a bad relationship or lose confidence if we are made redundant from a job we didn't like. We may still feel fractured and fragmented by the loss. Yet, paradoxically, we may also find it far harder to rebuild ourselves precisely because of the inauthentic nature of the relationships that we had. We may not fall so far when we lose something that was inauthentic, but we may find it harder to repair and to heal.

Conversely, we may be devastated when we lose an authentic and meaningful connection, and take considerable time to find our way out of grief. Yet, in the long term, having had that meaningful connection means that we are more likely to avoid resentment, to heal our fractured selves well, and to find a way to move forward with hope. When we make healthy connections, we lay a foundation for resilience.

Imagine a world in which we put our pursuit of recognition, material gain and a constant state of happiness aside, and instead, learn to celebrate healthy, meaningful connections within ourselves and within the immediacy of our social existence. A world in which we – wholeheartedly, bravely and compassionately – can be present in all weathers but can also let go of that which we lose. A world in which we learn to honour each day, good and bad, while always holding gratitude for the precious gift of life we have been given.

Living a Fierce Life

Living well is about living fiercely, with the conviction to make connections even when we know they can only ever be temporary. It is about having the courage to experience a broad range of authentic emotions as we ride the tide of our constantly changing existence. For most of us, there will be moments when we are truly filled with joy, when we declare that life is great. There will be other moments when we feel more mediocrity, feel sad or perhaps feel desperately distressed, and that is also OK. A fiercely lived, resilient life is a life filled with highs, lows and plenty of time walking the middle ground, from beginning to end.

So many of us yearn to stand out from the crowd, to be richer, wealthier and more highly lauded. Yet, it is those who learn to stand connected within the crowd, who grow to be the strongest.

Braving Loss

Still, the weight of loss can be incredibly hard to bear. So, how can we deal with the pain of losing our most important connections and then find the courage to make new ones in an authentic and meaningful way?

The first step is to understand the totality of who we are – all the way from our inner protective voice to the outermost layers of our social being. This helps us to develop deep awareness of how our identity develops and shifts in response to our experiences. We can then better understand how to embrace the best of life and how to honour, nurture and heal ourselves when tough times occur.

If we can build our 'whole-being' instead of trying to build 'resilience', resilience will be more accessible when we need it.

FOUR

Personal Identity – The Beginning of Becoming

IF WE WANT TO lead a life that feels authentic, real and whole, it helps immensely to know our inner voice. Moreover, if we want to be resilient when we lose a sense of ourselves, feel 'out of sorts' or completely broken, it helps if we first understand who we are beneath the fracture.

Our Inner Voice: Who We Are at Our Core

This means knowing our innermost self, beneath the socially constructed layers that make us a social being. Once we can experience a sense of our consistent inner voice, we can more easily find and heal ourselves when things go wrong. We are better equipped to know and pay attention to the strong, unbroken 'me' that lies within the seemingly fractured person we have become. The impenetrable 'me' that is there at our centre, defining the deepest, most consistent sense of ourselves as a human being. It is hard to live well as a person, experiencing the inevitable roller coaster of life, if we do not also know ourselves as a human being: self-knowing, self-accepting, surviving.

Unwrapping and 'seeing' this deep inner voice requires our time, our honesty, and putting judgement and self-criticism aside. It requires finding and acknowledging the deepest sense of who we are as a human, and what matters most to us, underneath the many socially created layers of our social identity.

Your inner voice is the most fundamental, foundational part of who you are as a living, cognisant, emotional being. A bright impenetrable jewel within you that is rolling through life, gathering the snow of time, experience and wisdom. Sometimes unknown and unseen, but ever present, driving your social development, and your sense of wholeness within the socially constructed world.

It is from our inner voice that our many socially created layers develop. From our basic understanding of the bipolarity of life, to our most important values, our self-beliefs, our morality and our judgements about ourselves and our world. It is these socially constructed layers that build us into an interactive, unique person.

The Golden Buddha of Wat Traimat

An ancient Buddhist tale from 1781 describes how Thai monks in Bangkok covered a giant gold statue of the Buddha with clay to protect it from Burmese invasion. The monks were all killed in the invasion, and the secret of the hidden golden Buddha was lost with them for almost three centuries. During this time, the clay statue was considered unremarkable and remained largely ignored. Eventually, in 1955, the statue had to be moved. As it was lifted, it fell. A large chip of clay was knocked off, revealing the shiny gold beneath. Immediately, the Thai community was compelled to remove the rest of the clay and to uncover the precious gold in full. The shining Golden Buddha now sits in the temple of Wat Traimat as one of the largest tourist attractions in Thailand.

This story offers us a metaphor for the covering of our true unencumbered self with the many layers of social construction that both trap us and construct us as people. As our socially created sense of ourselves takes hold, we easily forget our inner shining voice. A voice that is as beautiful as it is unencumbered by the need to manage an impression, avoid judgement or seek approval. If something serious happens to us, the resulting fracture to our socially constructed self can reveal our voice within. Perhaps we are knocked over by the death of someone we love, a messy divorce or a health scare. It is in these darkest moments that we may catch a glimpse of who we are at our core.

Consider your own life experiences. Can you recall a significant moment when your inner voice spoke to you? Perhaps it was a time when you said something that resonated with your whole being, and you knew, one hundred per cent, that this was something completely true for you, all the way to your core. Or perhaps it was a time when you took action, turned to head in a different direction, and the relief you felt was palpable.

The story of the golden Buddha suggests that, once we have been reminded of this inner voice, we will no longer be content to live without acknowledging it fully. From that moment on, we seek to rebuild ourselves as an authentic being.

When we are aware of our inner voice within our socially constructed self, we can respect ourselves 'to the core'. We can find peace with ourselves, even during times of turmoil. This inner voice then provides an anchor for us when we feel lost or are reeling from adversity.

Knowing our inner voice also ensures we can connect and reconnect with the external world in a way that feels genuine, raw and real. We can work to build congruence between it, and our socially created sense of who we are as a person: the clay layers with which we surround ourselves. We can nurture genuine self-acceptance and self-compassion. We can establish and honour our emotional boundaries with greater conviction and nurturing. This does not mean always feeling happy and, certainly, it doesn't mean that things are always going to go our way. Yet, no matter what tragedy happens, if we are authentically and meaningfully connected to our inner voice, we can be resilient when we need to, and heal.

Finding Your Inner Voice

So how do we find this inner voice? This golden jewel within our layered, social selves?

The answer, in itself, is not difficult, but the execution may be challenging to some. To find your core self, your inner voice, you need to learn to be still, physically and mentally. This may sound simple, but in our world of busy thoughts, and constant movement, it can be deceptively hard to know how to begin to do this.

This may mean the regular practising of guided mindful meditation or taking time to sit and breathe and to simply be quiet, for a few minutes a day, for every day you can manage it.

This is, of course, far easier said than done.

I recently noticed an article offering 'ten ways to achieve wellbeing that are not meditation'. It caught my attention because meditation, contemplation and reflection are so fundamentally valuable in my life. Still, I absolutely appreciate that if you have just been hit with a metaphorical truck, you may well feel more than a little skeptical about the idea of 'the power of sitting still'. There is an undeniable swirling energy that arises in pain. Even when we feel incapacitated in terms of our ability to get anything done or engage with the world, we are caught in a frenzy of internal emotion and stress. Thus, asking a traumatised person to learn calmness can be akin to presenting a red rag to a bull. At best, a session of mindfulness can seem like a Band-aid offered to a gaping wound.

Still, the power of consciously bringing our attention to the present is not to be underestimated and certainly not an activity to be confined to hippy communities or middle-aged middle-class women. If we can learn to become more self-aware, even for a moment, our inner turmoil will lessen. We will feel more centred, more able to cope. We will begin to recognise our inner calm voice, and it will begin to look after us.

The Simplest Plan is Often the Best Plan

There is a lot of money to be made from tangible ten step plans that sell well, and a lot of demand for concrete solutions to intangible problems, such as the pain caused by adversity and loss. Perhaps some people find the answers they are looking for in structured guides like these. But I believe the best long-term plans are often far less complex with far more depth.

In many ways, healthy mental practice is a bit like healthy eating. We can spend a fortune on diet books, strict eating regimes and group support, or we can simply focus on eating natural whole foods. It may initially seem more difficult to buy fresh ingredients and learn wholesome ways to cook them than 'simply' signing up for a low-calorie meal delivery service. However, understanding and learning healthy home cooking and eating is a more sustainable way to live than relying on others to prepare and deliver meals. It is certainly more in tune with our evolutionary journey, and more likely to lead to sustained positive change. In this sense, it is a case of playing the long game rather than seeking a 'quick fix'.

Simply put, meditating mindfully means taking time to sit quietly and observe your inner thoughts and feelings without trying to change them or engage with them. It is about observing the inner workings of your conscious mind; which means becoming more aware of who you are at your core.

It is a tough thing to do. I once listened to a revered Buddhist teacher talk about having an unprecedented opportunity to meditate with the Dalai Lama. An experience she had longed for ever since she discovered Buddhism as a spiritual path to wellbeing. Yet, when the time came and she found herself sitting next to the leader of the Buddhist world, she found herself pondering on whether or not she should get her hair cut shorter...or keep growing it.

After a few minutes lost in thought, this distracted teacher pulled herself back to the reality of her situation, in dismay. There she was meditating with one of the most well-known spiritual people in existence, and she was thinking about her hair. It was then that she realised how hard it is to stay in the moment and disengage with your thoughts, even when you really want to.

Being able to sit and be present without getting lost in a daydream or rumination is undeniably tough, partly because we are not used to sitting still with nothing or no-one to entertain or engage us. We may find ourselves immediately restless, distracted and caught up in thoughts we would rather not entertain. We may well find ourselves thinking about *not* thinking, and then become caught in the midst of a passing thought. We may also find ourselves wondering if all this trying to do nothing can really be doing anything at all. It can. It will.

Simple Meditation for the Skeptic

If you are very skeptical of meditation, inner stillness and 'the power of now', or skeptical of your ability to sit still without your thoughts taking over, then I suggest you set a low cost, simple goal: a goal that comes with a minimal expense of your time and energy, as well as negligible financial cost. Try being still for just five minutes a day for two weeks and see what happens. As is the way with most psychological and social learning, the value is in the practice. Theoretical knowledge and, indeed, popular opinions are never going to be enough to instill true understanding or lasting change.

I personally find it easiest to get healthy habits out of the way as early as possible in the day. This means taking your five or ten minutes as soon as you wake up, before checking Instagram, your email or the news headlines; before attending to children or work timetables or feeding the dog.

Try setting your alarm ten minutes earlier and then set your timer for ten minutes of meditation practice. Sit comfortably (sitting up stops you drifting back to sleep), close your eyes and breathe. Feel the coolness of the air you breathe in, and the warmth of the air you breathe out.

Then, after a minute or two, observe the many thoughts that are undoubtedly filling your mind and vying to grab your attention. Don't try to challenge them or get rid of them. Don't feel defeated if you, too, are wondering about your hairstyle, what is on your check list for the day, or what is wrong in your life right now. Simply observe your thoughts and accept them. Try looking at them in your head and watch them dissolve. Then, return to observing your breath.

Notice your emotional experience, be it frustration, sadness or joy. Observe it, identify it but don't try to change it, challenge it or lose yourself in it. Take a deep breath as you need it and know that it is OK to feel whatever you feel.

Hear the sounds that come and go around you, feel the floor under your feet and the temperature of the air.

And when you inevitably find yourself lost in thought once more, come back to observing your breath once again without judgement.

Try committing to five to ten minutes of stillness a day, every day, for two weeks... and see what happens.

Even for those of us enthusiastic about meditation, it can still be challenging. If you prefer more structure or support in your quest for self-awareness, you are certainly not alone. Perhaps try one of the many mindfulness or meditation apps and courses, run online and off. I am a huge fan of Sam Harris' Waking Up app which offers a great online introduction course to mindfulness meditation, and I have found enormous value in attending, in person, guided meditation sessions which focus on either mindfulness and compassion, or simply on the practice of counting your breath.

After a week or two of practising, rather than continuing to be lost in our socially constructed world, we start to feel more alert and more aware. Colours appear more vivid, the world is brighter, and we feel more at peace with ourselves. This means we are starting to recognise our inner voice. We will then begin to cope more effectively – and less fearfully – with the impact of losing what matters. We feel more alive – and the more alive we feel, the more life feels worth living.

The Timeless Me

Through our life, superficial changes fall and rise within us, but there remains our inner voice. Consistent, calm, centred and always there. It is the 'me' that is timeless, wise beyond time, youthful beyond the passing of years. It is the 'me' that has always been there to evaluate and guide us to greater connection and greater survival. It is the 'me' that observes, that provides a helicopter viewpoint and offers perspective.

This core version of us is the 'me' that arrived when we were born, that is there to help us, to be us even when we feel we are lost.

Even in the toughest moments of my life, I have had that small precious part of 'me' present and knowing. Such as when I was assaulted as a teenager, when I went through a divorce in my twenties, and when I lost my father in my forties.

I am unsure if that inner voice is simply a manifestation of my genetic makeup, but it feels wiser and more knowing than that. It feels like a manifestation of the memories that are held in my DNA across generations. Perhaps it is no more than a pre-conscious sense of self, a product of our evolution, created to guide our conscious contextually driven self. Perhaps it is a whole lot more.

If there is an eternal life, or indeed reincarnation, I believe it is in this inner voice we all have, in the age-old knowing that we are born with. Ultimately, attempts to understand and describe our inner voice will always fall short, because it is a self that is constructed *before* we socially construct ourselves with language and experience. It is the facet of our identity not concerned with the opinions of others, and not contained, contaminated or created by them. A core sense of ourselves that is void of the bipolarity that guides our every conscious perception.

Our wellbeing requires that we know who we are, and this requires knowing our core identity, and our deepest layers of social construction.

Once we connect our social driven identity with our deepest values and with our core inner voice, we can become a more congruent and whole authentic self and lead a more connected life. This means we no longer live such a constant threat of the transient reality of life, the inconsistencies, or the pain. It means we can feel more connected internally and with the world, even when loss occurs. We are better able to experience ourselves as whole, even when some part of our self-definition is threatened or lost.

When we hold our hand in the world, we place the world in our hand.

FIVE

Person-ality – Joining the World

THE POWER OF OUR inner voice is undeniable because it is the centre of who we are as an individual. Yet, it is only the beginning of who we are in the world. We do not navigate life alone; rather, life is with others. We navigate the world as social beings, as people.

Our Socially Constructed Identity

As people, we have a socially constructed identity around our inner voice, we have the beliefs, attitudes, thoughts and feelings that come from our experiences as a member of our socially constructed reality. Simply put, we have a personality—a social identity. Our social identity is created by all the connections we have (and have had throughout our life) with other people, with the unwritten social norms that guide us and show us what 'normal' is, with the overt rules and laws of our communities, and with the physical places we find meaning within. When our connections with others are congruent with our deepest sense of ourselves, our inner voice, and our values, we experience belonging and engagement. This means we experience wellbeing.

Thus, to better know who we are, we need to understand how our identity gradually develops from self to social. We need to understand how we grow from the deeply knowing and protective inner voice we are born with and are forever trying to return to. We need to understand how we move from human being to person-ality: from core to created.

As soon as we are born, the process of our becoming a social being begins. Our core identity is layered with a social covering, shaped into a socially created self. We learn, categorise and compartmentalise our beliefs, thoughts, feelings and behaviours. We separate one part of our emerging identity from another, our body from our mind, our self from others. Our social identity formation begins with a sense of self versus other, right versus wrong, real versus imagined, friend versus foe. As we continue to establish ourselves as part of our social world, we develop our personality. Social layers envelop us, categorise and label us. Defining our beliefs about who we are in the socially created world.

Personality and The People Around Us

When we're born, others around us immediately pass judgement on us: 'Isn't he beautiful', 'Isn't she a great sleeper', 'He's such a good baby.' (Whatever that means.)

As a new infant, we experience each label, first through the looks of others, their changing vocal tones, their facial expressions, and their touch, and then through their spoken words. We gradually develop ideas about who we are as a member of the social world. Right from the very beginning, subconsciously as that brand new squishy baby, we begin to learn a set of beliefs about what the world is, how it works, and about how we are placed within it. We build an understanding about how we fit within the socially constructed context around us, in which we are being socially and emotionally constructed.

We develop values, opinions and social behaviours. We develop a social identity.

Throughout life we continue to develop our social identity around our core identity, to grow with layers and complexity as a social being, a slowly changing, multi-layered, complex person with a slowly changing presence in the world.

I love knowing that glass is a liquid. It seems amazing to me that the solid immovable-looking substance we see all around us is, in fact, slowly moving. I remember examining old windows in the English countryside as a child and noting that each pane was thicker at the bottom than at the top.

Slowly, around the world, windows are imperceptibly 'flowing' down towards the earth. Our social identity and personality remind me of glass. Panes of glass often appear solid, unmoving, set for life. Yet they are fluid and slowly changing. Retrospectively we can look back at our life and see how our socially created self has gently shifted and changed over time, while we felt more or less 'the same'.

As time passes, we all continue to change, slowly, imperceptibly... like glass flowing...

As we develop as a person, we develop our expression of who we are in the world, our person-ality.

Traits vs States

Much of the work trying to unpack and categorise personality has assumed that each personality is made up of a set number of fairly consistent characteristics. In fact, many researchers believe these characteristics to be traits, fixed ways of being and behaving that stand apart from context and experience. For example, we might say 'this person is always gregarious and a social butterfly' or 'that person is always shy and introverted'.

Some who study personality, including myself, suggest that it makes no sense to separate our personality from our environment. Rather, we suggest that personality comprises a set of changing ways of interacting with the world. These vary according to the variations in the contexts in which we find ourselves, and from which we develop. We suggest that personality is less about 'traits' and more about 'states'. For example, someone might be gregarious when out with friends but really shy in the staff room at work.

The Eysenck Personality Inventory

During the 1970s, academic psychologists became very interested in Hans Eysenck's personality inventory as a means of categorising and understanding personality with reference to first two and then three distinct dimensions: extroversion vs introversion, neuroticism vs emotional stability, and subsequently, psychoticism vs self-control. The profile describes each person's personality as a unique point in two-dimensional space. This point represents a quantifiable position on each of the three dimensions. For example, a person may be placed on the spectrum at a point more introvert than extrovert, more neurotic than emotionally stable and more self-controlled than psychotic. Thus, we would say that this person has a personality which is largely introverted, neurotic and controlled.

Although Eysenck's personality theory had many supporters, these were often people who believed that the theory identifies fixed personality 'traits', rather than the dynamic 'states' I believe in. They thought, for example, if the profile identified you as extroverted, you would be consistently extroverted whatever the circumstance. In contrast, state theorists like me believe that extroversion is contextually dependent. It could be that in most situations you behave in an extroverted way, but this personality expression is still dependent on the context: an extrovert might be less extroverted in certain situations.

Consider your own experiences with context. Can you imagine two differing settings that bring out contrasting aspects of your character and behaviour? Is there a context in which you are comfortable to be loud and extroverted, versus one in which you are more introverted and reserved? I know that I can be the first on the dance floor if I am celebrating during a night out with close friends, whereas I can barely feel able to speak at a school parents night event attended by other parents who I don't know very well.

I am glad to say that by the time I became familiar with Eysenck's work in the late 1980s, increasing numbers of academics had begun questioning his theory due to its failure to consider context. These critics suggested that although Eysenck's theory offers a way of defining a person's personality characteristics at any given time, our personality can and does indeed change across time and place. In support of this more contextually-supported view of personality, it has been suggested that any continuity in findings from personality profiling is representative of contextual consistency, rather than the immovable quality of personality per se. For example, a consistently anxious person could be said to be consistently anxious because they don't find a context that meets their needs more effectively, not because they were incapable of changing themselves. For example, despite working to positively change and develop, they may continue to spend time with people who do not effectively meet their needs, or persevere in a job that is unfulfilling, or live in a town that does not support their interests and political viewpoint.

I too, have come to believe, without doubt, that although we do indeed have a deep-seated core part of ourselves, our more visible social identity – our personality – slowly ebbs and flows with the contextual tide of time and experience. We may be quite shy as a young person, but then, as we gain confidence in ourselves and experience different social contexts such as jobs or friend groups, we may become more comfortable speaking to strangers.

So, in short: we each have a unique personality, but not an unchangeable one.

The Five-Factor Model

Another popular model of personality is commonly known as 'the five-factor model', originally presented by researchers Robert McCrae and Paul Costa in the 1980s and developed over many years by many others interested in personality. Unlike Eysenck's three dimensions, you can probably guess that the five-factor model proposes five factors. These are: openness, extraversion, conscientiousness, agreeableness and neuroticism.

Critics of the five-factor model, including myself, have similar concerns to those of the opponents of Eysenck's personality theory. Most notably, we argue that when we 'average' a person's responses over many situations, we end up with an assessment of their personality that minimalises the influence of context, and the possibilities for growth and change.

Imagine Tom, a ten-year-old boy who is teased daily. Tom rarely responds aggressively to being teased despite it happening frequently. Now imagine Jack, another ten-year-old boy. Jack is rarely teased about anything however, if ever he is, he responds aggressively every time. These two children might act aggressively an equivalent number of times over the course of a year, leading some to suggest that their behaviour patterns—or even their personalities—are equivalent. However, I propose that Tom and Jack appear to be two very different children, with two very different sets of contextual experience, and two very different ways of expressing themselves in the world. Here, the context is very important in understanding both children.

To assume that our social identity is fixed from situation to situation, and across time, limits our potential for personal growth and complexity, and for finding deep meaning and purpose in life.

Changing the Context

'State' theories place our personality in the hands of our context as well as 'in us' as individuals. In so doing, state theorists suggest that it is indeed possible to change and develop our personality. Moreover, if we want to feel or act differently in life, as much as we might work to change ourselves, we might also consider changing our context, and shift where we live, work or play. For example, we might want to change our social groups, our jobs or even potentially move from our current home. Mindfulness teacher and author Jon Kabat-Zinn introduced the notion: 'Wherever we go, we take ourselves with us' in his 1994 book 'Wherever You Go There You Are'. Kabat-Zinn suggests that, when we want to become happier, we gain more by working on ourselves rather than on changing our environment. I believe it would be more accurate to suggest that 'wherever we go, like glass flowing, we gradually become someone new'. This is why, when a young adult goes to university, the people who know them best will see changes to their personality when they come home for visits: their context has changed and they're learning new skills while developing a new relationship with the world.

Our social identity changes and matures because of the changing influence of all the contexts in which we live and connect. In a broad 'horizontal' sense, this happens across the different places, cultures and communities in which we spend time. It also happens through the passage of time as we age. Both across different situations and through the passage of time, each contextual experience gradually shapes and makes us into someone new.

The Power of Language

Our language is a powerful voice for our contextual experiences, and deeply influences how we understand ourselves, how we see the world, and how we express ourselves within it. In many ways our personalities represent the language we learn and use.

Many English women of my mother's generation were shaped with a language that spoke of 'duty', 'family responsibility', 'shame' and 'stoicism' along with a determination to 'always present with a smile'. With age and experience on their side, I have learned much from my mother's English cohort. They were all born in the 1930s and early 1940s and were undeniably influenced by a Victorian legacy and the horrors of World War II. Many of these older ladies have also developed a great perspective along with the realisation that life is best lived in the details of every moment. My mother and her friends help me to maintain my own perspective, find calm in every storm, and never take life too seriously.

In contrast, my Australian daughters' generation appears to be more shaped by 'a yearning for recognition', 'a call for perfectionism' and teenaged 'entitlement' along with an expectation of 'equality', 'opportunity' and the freedom to be more socially and emotionally visible in the world. My daughters benefit from much talk about the increased rights for women that shaped them from birth. However, their immersion in the language of social media and advertising makes them prey to insidious social comparison and a constant fear of missing out. Everyday my teenaged children teach me about standing up for myself, staying curious and speaking out. They also help me to avoid the cynicism of my own place in time, that of middle age.

When we are young, the language of our context has a powerful influence over how we see ourselves and how we interact with the world, simply because we have had fewer experiences to already influence us. The older we become, the more complex we become, and the less each new message is likely to change us. In this, our personality may indeed begin to become more 'trait like'. When we are older, we have increasingly meshed layers built around us, forged through time and experience. We are less likely to notice a shift in our personality when we experience a significant contextual change.

Still, even for the most established of us, deep change can and does occur. A significant change can cut through many layers of social identity, especially when it impacts something upon which our deepest sense of self is built. If this happens due to the loss of a loved one, or the loss of something that really matters to our self-definition, we become fractured, and need time to repair.

At other times, major change is welcome. It can enlighten us in our journey to create a meaningful life; and to connect with a world that supports our needs. We may fall in love, discover a new passion, or experience a deeply profound moment of self-realisation.

Change changes us for better or worse. Sometimes like a beaming ray of sunlight, at other times like a long, perhaps miserable walk in the rain.

The Problem with 'Character'

In more recent times, interest has shifted from considering personality per se, to considering the specific aspects of personality that are believed to be desirable for leading a 'good life'. As someone who believes that the pursuit of happiness is akin to living a half-life, I find this positive skewing to be unnerving. As I describe in Chapter One, I believe that we need to embrace the enjoyable and desirable hand in hand with the difficult and unwanted aspects of life; as we move through a continuous cycle of identity formation, fracture and reparation.

Yet, many supporters of the 'positive psychology' movement of the 2000s have embraced Martin Seligman and Christopher Peterson's ideas of 'character strengths' as a central tenet of defining our best selves. Seligman and Peterson suggest that, not only can we define ourselves by a mix of 'traits' rather than 'states', but that some of these traits are inherently more desirable than others. They go on to purport that there are 24 different character traits that contribute to the 'positive' side of our personality and they call these 'character strengths'. Although they suggest we possess all 24-character strengths to a greater or lesser degree, they also state that we each have a 'top five', irrespective of our age or experience.

It is worth noting that the 24 character 'strengths' identified by Seligman and Peterson were identified from the very social contexts in which we are all created and defined. They come from cultural references, commonly used phrases and even from greeting cards. There is, therefore, an implicit nod to the contextual creation of each aspect of personality. Yet, when looking to identify these 'strengths' in individuals, limited recognition has been given to the role of context in engendering their ongoing development or use.

As someone who believes that the value of any belief of behaviour is only judgeable within the context in which it occurs, I am immediately concerned by the concept of 'character strengths' as positive aspects of being and behaving that are held within us. Once again, we are being encouraged to consider the way we express ourselves within our changing world as independent of that world, even though it was developed within it.

Context is Key

Certainly, there are some aspects of character which work well for us in most contexts, most of the time. For example, I would be pushed to identify many situations in which it is inappropriate or unhelpful to be kind, curious or enthusiastic. Similarly, I am confident there are expressions of character which are destructive and demoralising in most contexts: selfishness, disinterest and arrogance. Still, there is no single way of being or behaving that is *always* the best way to be or behave, in every situation, at every time. Moreover, there are many expressions of personality that work well to support healthy connections in some contexts but are heavily problematic in others.

For example, if a socially anxious employee gives a presentation in front of their peers in the boardroom, we can positively reflect on the courage they have brought to the situation. If someone forgives their partner forgetting their birthday, we can suggest they demonstrated high levels of forgiveness and compassion. Courage enables a nervous presenter to share their work in a safe environment; compassion and forgiveness enable a healthy relationship to prosper when a partner makes mistakes. However, despite often being virtuous, the value of the characteristics each person brings to each situation are still dependent on the situation.

These same attitudes and behaviours may prove to be less helpful in a different situation. For example, a person choosing to walk along a high wall with a serious risk of falling off has also shown 'courage', as did our nervous presenter; however, we could call their behaviour fool-hardy or downright crazy in this situation. Courage is not a 'strength' in this context. Similarly, someone who forgives their partner for being violent towards them is demonstrating deep levels of 'compassion', but arguably not in a healthy or safe way in this context. Thus, strength of character is about employing the most effective and useful attitudes, beliefs and behaviours within any given context; which is very different to simply having 'character strengths' per se.

Moreover, I would describe as limiting and dangerous the idea of judging aspects of personality to be either positive (strengths) or negative (non-strengths).

'Limiting', in that different contexts support and encourage different ways of being and different ways of connecting. 'Dangerous', because it supports the notion of there being a hierarchy of preferred personality traits, which opens the gates to competition, comparison and judgement. I fear that we will one day be choosing schools for our children where the students attain the highest scores for wellbeing and character or show the most coveted combinations of 'character strengths'. League wellbeing tables would, in my mind, be a terrifying thing.

In summary, no way of being or behaving is inherently worthy of judgement when considered without context. Human behaviour takes on positive or negative connotations when we consider them within a specific context: within a specific culture, time and place. Once we consider context, we can better understand any attitude or behaviour as helpful or unhelpful, healthy or unhealthy, useful or useless. No way of being or behaving is inherently good or bad: it is the context that makes it so.

I believe our personality is more helpfully understood as a collection of socially constructed states than a collection of immovable traits.

SIX

Authenticity

IF WE CAN LEARN to live with balance and harmony between our inner-most voice, our deepest values, our socially constructed layers and our ongoing interaction with the world, our life feels whole and authentic. Simply put: living well means ensuring our inner voice and our core values align with our socially constructed self; who we are as a person. When we are aligned from the deepest sense of who we are to the most outward expression of ourselves, we feel wholly connected to the world; we feel internally whole. We feel we belong; we feel at our most alive. We can live life in a way that feels authentic, meaningful and real.

My mid-twenties represented a very low point in my life, but also a transformative experience. Thinking back to the story of the stunning metamorphosis of the hidden golden Buddha of Wat Traimit, I can definitely say that a significant emotional fall provided an opportunity for me to reconnect with my own inner voice.

Waking Up to Myself

At just 22 years old, in an impulsive and defiant move, I married my decidedly wayward boyfriend. He had captivated me with his undeni-able intelligence and charisma, but the relationship was chaotic and tumultuous at best. He was a man of exceptional potential, but was enslaved by a need to disrupt and push against anything that resembled a rule. Our breaking point came when he sold a large amount of marijuana to some of our student friends, and was sent to prison for six weeks for his efforts.

His arrest made the local news.

After two weeks of me crying over my husband's custodial absence, a friend visited with a video for me to watch. He suggested it might help. It not only helped: it completely changed my life.

My desperate moment suddenly became an unexpected opportunity to wake up to myself. It was the chance I needed to re-engage with my inner voice, and to find the courage to leave my husband. This meant finding the courage to finally break free from an unhappy life and to become a better, more authentic me.

The video called 'The Power of Myth' comprised a series of talks between interviewer Bill Moyers and the mythologist and philosopher Joseph Campbell. To this day, I quote Campbell's ideas with incessant regularity; and lead a life both personally and professionally that is shaped by his words. Most notably, he helped me to understand that *a meaningful life is about feeling alive*, rather than finding any secret for being happy or avoiding trauma.

There is no magical key to unlocking wellbeing, no ultimate pot of happiness at the end of a multicoloured search. Campbell taught me that feeling well is all about connecting to life in the here and now, in an authentic and meaningful way. And this is all about knowing and honouring the inner voice of who you are; and all you can be.

Sam Harris tells us that we do not meditate to become good at meditation, rather, we meditate to wake up to our life. How true.

Closing your eyes in meditation can help you to find your inner voice but then you need to take note: you need to also intentionally honour that self you have found, with your eyes open.

Campbell famously said that when you do something that you authentically and honestly connect to, something that makes you feel truly alive, you need to hold onto it. I believe he was saying that it is important to follow your dreams, but not romantic dreams of salvation. Rather, dreams that reflect your values and inner voice. Dreams that lead to you becoming more of who you are, rather than being someone different.

Sam Harris is saying the same thing, but in a different way. He believes that meditation gives us the doorway to seeing ourselves and our lives clearly and distinctly so that we connect more fully to life; so that we more readily develop a sense of belonging.

Finding My Voice

Back in 1990, less than a month after my rebellious husband returned home from jail, I realised that our unhealthy relationship was not going to change. More importantly, I knew that I was never going to be able to nurture myself while in it.

I remember getting up one Saturday morning about 9:00am, feeling tired and emotional. I sat alone in the tiny living room of our one-bedroom home, tears streaming down my face. I was no longer able to hold my emotions back and find any semblance of outward control.

Around noon, my husband appeared from the bedroom, dressed and ready to head out. I had hardly seen him for days. He looked at me sobbing on the couch. Then, with impatience, and exasperation in his voice, he asked: 'What is wrong with you?'

Even though I knew he was putting me down, rather than really asking a question, I replied.

'I'm leaving.'

As the words tumbled from my mouth, I knew they were the truest words I had spoken for a very long time.

For me, learning about authenticity and belonging began with changing my context dramatically. I had to find the courage to leave, so that I could find the courage to make my way home.

Authentic connection between our most inner voice and our most outward behaviours is the essence of belonging. It is also the antithesis of impression management. Impression management literally means 'managing the impression of ourselves we present to others'. For example, this might mean dressing a certain way, acting cheerfully even if you do not feel cheerful, or even pretending to hold certain attitudes or like certain activities. We tend to consciously manage our impression when we are trying to impress other people to comply, avoid criticism, or to please. Research professor and best-selling author Brené Brown helps us to realise this when she talks about the problem of impression management, and how it results in our trying to change ourselves to fit a situation and be accepted. In her best-selling book *The Gifts of Imperfection* Brown writes: 'Fitting in is about assessing a situation and becoming who you need to be to be accepted. Belonging, on the other hand, doesn't require us to change who we are; it requires us to be who we are.' In contrast, when we experience belonging, we are honouring the deepest sense of ourselves while connecting to the situation around us. Once we connect to a social context in this authentic way, we internalise the norms of that context and become part of something both meaningful and bigger than ourselves. In many ways, becoming part of something bigger than ourselves is what gives our lives purpose, and thus it is vital for our overall wellbeing, and for our capacity to be resilient when times are tough.

Living authentically is about both being and doing. It is about making connections with our world in a way that is congruent with our inner voice and deepest values. It is about engaging and being passionate about being curious. It is about feeling alive.

When adversity and trauma come knocking, our ability to live authentically ensures we can still have a sense of who we are, even as we acknowledge our fractured identity, take time to heal and move through our grief.

Living authentically can be painful and risky at times, but it is the only path to long-term resilience and being a whole being.

SEVEN

Life is with Others

SOME WOULD SAY THAT when thinking about how best to live authentically, establishing healthy relationships with others is everything. Certainly, the quality and quantity of the relationships we have with other people matter greatly. It matters that we have relationships with people which feel accepting, energising, vulnerable, supportive, kind and caring.

As social beings who generally reside in groups, our relationships with others need to be understood more broadly than simply the one-to-one relationships we have with individuals. Our relationships with people are also about our relationships to whole groups. We might say 'I get along well with Jack' or 'I can't stand Jonathan'; we may also say 'I love this group' or 'I am really struggling with the team'.

Relationships with others matter – be it as individuals or within groups.

Knowing ourselves is a vital first step to creating meaningful connections with others, but it is not the only step.

Nor is it enough to admire or love another person or to simply want to be connected to them socially and emotionally, although these aspects of relationship building are undoubtedly vitally important.

The Four Key Ways of Being in Relationship

Making connections with others requires the appropriate knowledge and skills to meet other peoples' needs, as well as our own; these skills are necessary to ensure we can create meaningful connections that are mutually supportive, sustainable, flexible and strong. As I am only too aware, this is all far harder said than achieved.

I believe that our connections to others strengthen and grow when we focus on four key ways of being, to utilise in our day-to-day social web building.

1. Being present
2. Being kind
3. Being curious
4. Being inclusive

Being Present

Knowing how to be 'positively present' is arguably the most fundamentally important skill for building a meaningful connection with anyone. It involves knowing how to listen, without judgement, how to pay attention, and how to care.

We like others when we believe they are hearing and seeing us in a way which feels accepting of the way we want to be heard and seen. We do not like others who tell us what to do, or who to be. Furthermore, we do not like others who use our turn to talk to think about what they want to say next. Certainly, we may sometimes ask someone for advice, but we rarely appreciate advice when it is unsolicited and shrouded in judgement. Rather, we want others to hear us, accept us, and help us to know we are lovable, just as we are.

Thus, learning to be present is also about learning acceptance and how to embrace others without trying to change or 'improve' them.

Three years ago, I bought a new car. It was quite a bit bigger and more powerful than my previous car had been. I loved it. Still, it did take a bit of getting used to – the different controls, the wider dimensions and its higher riding position. About two weeks after I got it, I found myself carefully trying to park behind another very new looking but much smaller vehicle. It was a manoeuvre I'd done countless times before in decades of driving. I remember my foot slipping as I reached for the brake, and to my horror, I accidentally accelerated into the back of the shiny boot in front of me. The awful sound of crunching metal was accompanied by my screeching loudly.

Easily done hey.

Apparently not.

At least not according to Neil when I sheepishly relayed what had happened. He asked me if I needed to perhaps rethink large car ownership...or take a formal lesson or two in parking.

I did not receive this feedback well.

Later the same day, I recounted the accident to a good friend. My friend listened without offering advice or judgement, and I immediately felt better. She then cheerfully told me how she had driven her new car into the side of her house by mistake, several years previously.

I ended the conversation feeling accepted, capable and far happier. Pressing the accelerator instead of the brake had not exactly been normalised as an acceptable behaviour, but *I* felt normal again, and very grateful to my friend for listening so well.

In Neil's defence, it can be really hard not to tell someone what to do if you think you have an answer to offer. Supporting others in times of need could be compared to watching someone in a play who has excruciatingly forgotten their lines. Rather than shout out the line or jump to the stage to finish the performance for them, far better to offer patience, your continued presence and your faith in their ability to find a way to finish their performance themselves.

We need to continually learn how to place ourselves enthusiastically and supportively in the front row for other's stories, while doing our best to stay off their stage.

Being Kind

One of the greatest facets of any healthy relationship, and indeed, any cohesive culture, is kindness. Kindness is, therefore, understandably valued highly in most cultures and societies. Yet all too often, our desire to make a good impression to a distant crowd prevents us from considering the needs of those who stand closest.

In today's celebrity-driven world, many people see being famous as indistinguishable from being infamous. It is not so much what you do that seems to count, as much as how many people know about it. As such, we live in a time of impression management at the expense of authentic accomplishments and developing true belonging. This has resulted in many of us, young and old, believing that relationships are formed when you impress someone – even if at the expense of someone else – rather than understanding that it is far more important to learn to be kind and to develop authentic relationships with other kind people.

Kindness is far more than a behaviour. We cannot encourage kindness simply by acknowledging or rewarding 'helping behaviours' that *appear* to be kind. Rather, true kindness is an act that stems from an intention to benefit someone else. It is born from empathy and compassion, certainly not from a desire for approval and praise.

The best way we can support kindness in others is by genuinely being kind ourselves. The more we are authentically and sincerely kind to others, the stronger our relationships will become with them, and the kinder they will be to us. Not only does kindness connect us through our intentions and behaviour, it builds understanding and acceptance. As such, we like others more when we are kind to them, and they like us more when they demonstrate kindness to us.

To be genuinely kind to others, we need to first accept that everyone is doing their best to survive, to be seen and to belong. As soon as we are willing to accept that everyone we meet is doing their best to find their voice in the world, we can start to develop greater compassion – and demonstrate genuine kindness – towards them. This does not mean we have to like or love everyone. Nor does it mean that we need to give ourselves to everyone emotionally or socially or take their stresses and distress onto ourselves. Boundaries are important and indeed essential for our own wellbeing. Rather, living kindly means continually and consistently communicating with care and compassion for both others and for ourselves.

Being present and being kind are vitally important for supporting meaningful relationships and wellbeing. Yet, if we are struggling with trauma and adversity, all aspects of relationship development can seem far more challenging. For example, living through the COVID pandemic created enormous stress for many of us, which may have lowered our social and emotional capacity to be present, to care, and, indeed, to be consistently kind.

Many of us found that as lockdowns and border closures continued, we were less consistently calm, less open to others' points of view, less patient, less understanding. This all means that when we interacted with others, we needed to ensure we remained aware of our own stress levels and also remembered to be kind to ourselves.

Just as it helps to know that others are doing the best they can, we need to ensure we take time to know that we are doing the best we can, especially if we are navigating turbulent times. If we can do this, we can cultivate greater self-acceptance, focus more on self-care and ensure we meet our own needs for wellbeing as well as supporting the needs of others.

Being Curious

We develop positive relationships more strongly when we take time to get to know each other beyond the reason for our initial connection. The process begins with simple but powerful steps such as asking work colleagues how their weekend was (and taking the time to listen to their answer); taking an interest in a grandparent's life history; or asking a child how they are before suggesting they tidy their room. In this way, positive connections arise from a genuine, caring, curiosity and interest in others.

Across the developed world, there has been a lot of emphasis lately on developing an interest and caring curiosity in others' wellbeing. This is often summed up with a reminder to ask others: 'Are you OK?' Although it is important to destigmatise poor mental health and encourage open conversation about social and emotional wellbeing, I am unsure how effective this question really is.

Across much of the developed world, we greet others every day with 'How are you?' Asking someone if they are OK is therefore not necessarily seen as a question that requires an answer. This means, when we want to genuinely ask someone how they are, we can benefit greatly from asking *twice*. The first time we inquire, we are in effect saying a culturally acceptable hello. The second time, we are taking the time to ask because we genuinely want to know how they are faring in their lives, and we are signalling that we will be really listening to the reply.

Being Inclusive

Connection can be further developed with others through commonality and the celebration of shared interests, humour and experiences.

One benefit of the online communications we've seen become more common throughout the pandemic has been the sense of familiarity and vulnerability it has highlighted between people. We have seen hilarious Zoom recordings of executives floored by their young children surprising them in 'important' meetings, including the famous BBC live TV interview when Professor Robert Kelly, delving into the nuances of South Korean politics, was interrupted by his toddler. Glimpses of other people's homes have intrigued us as they meet with us online. Even popular culture has been beamed into our living rooms, with some musical acts offering customised concert experiences as we whiled away the isolation. Although pandemic life separated us physically, it also provided new windows for connection at a very human level.

As we learned during the pandemic: when it comes to resilience, wellbeing matters, and that means other people matter a lot.

Learn to be present, be kind, be curious, be inclusive.

Consider the qualities in others that make the people you feel safe with, loved by and nurtured around. Who are the people who support you feeling good about yourself? What is it they are doing to make your time with them so desirable?

Once we have the self-awareness, acceptance, an understanding of others, and good relationship skills, we can build a strong web to hold us in life, even when times are tough.

EIGHT

Context Counts

THE PREVIOUS CHAPTER EMPHASISES the importance of relationships with other people. Certainly, our relationships with others provide a vital way for us to connect to our contexts. Still, they are not the only way we connect to our context. As such they are not the only way we define ourselves as social beings, nor are they the only way our context meets our core needs. For example, if I asked you to tell me about your family, you may well begin by telling me about the other people within it. But then there would be more.

You may also tell me where your family are from, culturally and geographically. You may tell me what they are like in terms of the rules and the norms they abide by, the rituals and practices they follow, the values they uphold. You would describe the social context of your family with attention to several aspects of context.

Certainly, if I were to describe my family of origin, I would include a reference to growing up with two parents and two brothers but there would be far more to my description than a list of people, their personalities and their relationships with each other. I would describe the small village of Themelthorpe where we all lived throughout my childhood. I would talk about our 'English-ness', and our being polite and reserved much of the time. I would detail some of the rituals we shared daily, such as eating a family meal around the table, and always saying goodnight in a certain way. I would also mention how we could be pretty competitive with each other, how we siblings grew up to live around the world, but ultimately how we are all unquestioningly available should an emergency arise. I would describe a social context that was more than the people within it.

Moving to Australia

Whenever I am asked why I moved from the UK to live and work in Australia in my early thirties, I always struggle to provide an honest explanation. Especially one that is coherent and complete. In many ways, the reasons I emigrated have changed as I have grown older and changed myself, a kind of revisionism if you will.

As much as Australia is indeed an amazing country in so many ways, there was no magical enlightening moment waiting for me at Sydney airport when I landed. I was quick to discover both the truth and the lie in the adage: wherever we travel, we take ourselves along for the ride.

When I arrived in Australia, there I still was, at least in the beginning. No more glamorous or self-assured just because I had taken the leap to try to expand my geographical or social horizons. My personal identity was still right there with me on day one. It takes time to internalise a new context and change.

I was also to discover how powerfully and fully I had internalised the norms of English life, the details and the virtues of the world I had just left behind. When I arrived in Australia, there I no longer was.

I arrived in a country separated by a common language and was soon to become painfully aware that I was not a self-contained individual simply hopping from one context to another. Rather I was a product of more than thirty years of English life, and my social identity had been deeply entwined with all things English. I am not a rolling stone but rather I am flowing like glass, gathering and growing my identity as I slowly pour down the hill of my life.

It took a long time for me to plunge into Australian life and to stop resisting my inevitable change. My fear of my new country was not simply confined to meeting new people. It was about the culture, Australian norms, rules and attitudes; and about the physical environment around me...especially the tropical wildlife.

I quickly became convinced it was a miracle that anyone had made it to adulthood in my new neigbourhood, when so much of the fauna seemed poised to kill me outright.

I feared the toxic box jellyfish, the ridiculously sized spiders and the threat of sharks. I was fearful of large frilly necked lizards looking like inhabitants of Jurassic Park. I was terrified of all the different species of snakes. I was even nervous of the beautiful green tree frogs and the child-friendly stick insects. Heaven forbid anyone had mentioned Australians favourite mythical pests: Drop Bears.

When I first arrived in Queensland, I found an apartment opposite the beach, which fitted neatly with my Australian dream. My balcony looked out on calm crystal-clear blue waters lapping around rocky outcrops; gently greeting the endless white sandy beach with long lingering laps. It all looked a lot like my imaginings of Paradise. Unfortunately, it didn't feel much like I imagined Paradise to be, once I was living in the view.

I had to walk through ten metres of rough scrub land and grasses to reach the picture-perfect beach from the road that ran in front of my apartment. Not a big deal, but immediately a massive challenge once I had been warned to keep an eye out for sand pythons. Although not venomous, sand pythons are very different animals to the cute little squirrels I was used to in Sheffield. I was so scared of encountering one of these enormous snakes, the scrubby crossing became a walk of abject terror each time I attempted to get to the beach. I tried walking slowly and tentatively forward. I tried taking a long walk around the extensive scrub to avoid the crossing altogether. I tried taking two massive leaps, which always turned into three. And finally, I settled on a fast run without looking at all.

In those first few months, I avoided getting my mail for a week because a green tree frog had temporarily made my letterbox into her home. I frantically scratched bites from tiny sand flies that passed easily through my fly screens (I had scars on my ankles for 12 months). I also took hundreds of photos of colourful parrots, excited and delighted to see them flying freely.

In addition to the climate and wildlife, I met the daily challenge of learning to understand and connect with Australian people. We were indeed separated by a common language. When the head of the psychology department invited me to a BBQ and asked me to bring along a 'plate', I thought he must not have enough crockery for all the guests, and so arrived at his home with a plate...an empty one. Of course, he had meant for me to bring a plate of food.

During those first months, I realised there is all the difference in the world between going somewhere on holiday and moving somewhere to live. When on holiday you can view all sorts of differences in the world around you, knowing you will then return home to report back to others and indulge in sharing a perspective on a different place. When you move somewhere to live, it becomes so important to not only be aware of different cultural norms, different cultural rules, different people and different physical places. It is also vital to learn to understand them, learn to connect with them and ultimately to internalise them until they become your own.

The Four Domains of Social Context

I believe that every aspect of any social context can be considered within four intertwined domains. These absolutely include the people but they also acknowledge the policy and practices set out in the rules and laws within the context, the social norms that silently guide the people and provide them with an unspoken belief in 'how the world works', and the physical space in which the context exists.

The Four Domains of Context that Support Contextual Wellbeing, Street, 2018

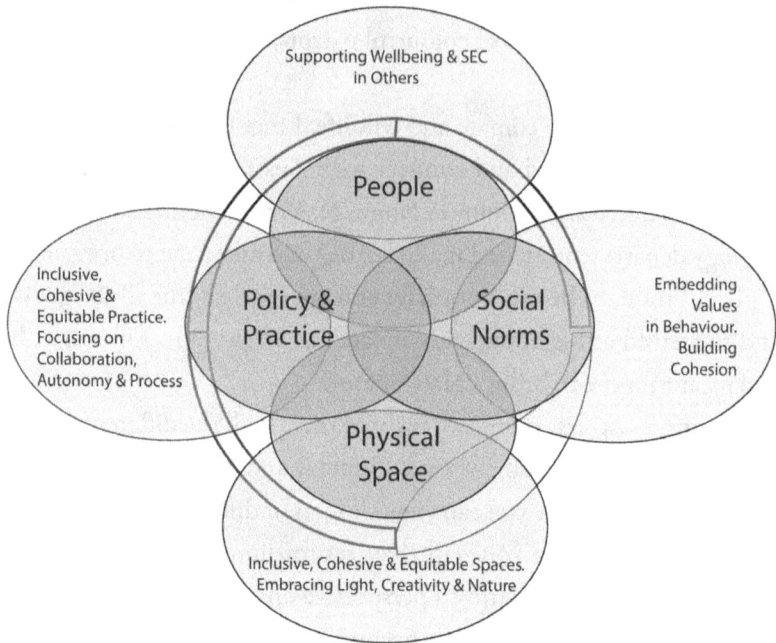

Supporting Wellbeing & SEC in Others

People

Inclusive, Cohesive & Equitable Practice. Focusing on Collaboration, Autonomy & Process

Policy & Practice

Social Norms

Embedding Values in Behaviour. Building Cohesion

Physical Space

Inclusive, Cohesive & Equitable Spaces. Embracing Light, Creativity & Nature

Domain One – Relationships with Others

As explored in Chapter Seven, our relationships with others are undoubtedly powerful and important. I won't repeat the sentiment of the previous chapter here, but it emphasises the power and the importance of others in our lives; as do many other chapters in the book.

As some might say, the three greatest contributors for wellbeing are relationships, relationships and relationships.

Domain Two – Policy and Practice – The Rules of Engagement

We also experience wellbeing when we willingly connect to and follow the rules of the groups and communities in which we find ourselves;

and these rules support our key three needs (which we will explore in Chapter Eleven).

Policy and practice are overtly known as rules for everyday behaviour within any given context or community. They refer to the written policies detailing the laws and the local rules of our communities, big and small. For example, this includes universal government rules to always drive under a certain speed in built up areas, or a family rule to keep our feet off the coffee table at home. However, unlike social norms, rules do not necessarily guide our attitudes or reflect the *actual* behaviour of all people, all the time. For example, many adults will occasionally, if not regularly, drive faster than the official rule allows. Many family members may put their feet on the prized coffee table when no one is watching.

Domain Three – Social Norms – The Way Life Is

Social norms are the unwritten rules that guide our actual behaviour. They are internalised in us and are part of our social identity. We do not often consider them consciously, but we adhere to them and use them to understand our manufactured world and to guide our social behaviour.

For example, in the western world we often put out a hand to shake the hand of another person when meeting for the first time. This has long been a socially constructed greeting that we participate in automatically, and certainly without much question as to why we are doing it. The pandemic has forced us to challenge and change this and other ingrained social norms due to health concerns. As challenging as the pandemic has been, it has also provided an opportunity to 'see' what norms we are following and to experience how odd and uncomfortable it feels to *not* follow them.

It took time for many western communities to adjust to not shaking hands, hugging or sitting too close to others. But over time, these new pandemic-driven behaviours have become more established and consequently feel more 'normal'. I recently heard someone saying it felt 'odd' to go out without a mask. A sure sign of the relentless long-term nature of COVID restrictions.

Social norms stem from group values or rules and develop through repetition. Some social norms simply help us to have more capacity when engaging in social activities. For example, the social norms to sit at a table in a restaurant and to order a savoury main course before we consider a sweet dessert, all work to help us have an established plan for going out for dinner. A plan which we follow without much thought or attention but one that ensures we have capacity and energy for other things such as making conversation and enjoying our meal.

Other norms are more concerned with our attitude and approach to how we understand our place and participation in the community. For example, a norm to keep our front door always locked may well be built on a belief in our lack of safety in our community, and the dishonesty of certain other people. A norm to invite our friends into our home and offer them dinner is likely to be built on a belief that we need to welcome and support those we care about.

Healthy social norms support equity because they support the needs of all members of any given context, rather than just a privileged few. They generally include being honest and trustworthy, being respectful to others and supporting other's place in a community, as well as our own.

Domain Four – Physical Spaces – From Spaces to Places

The social context also includes the physical spaces in which we find ourselves. The physical spaces we exist in contribute to our social construction of reality and, consequently, to our social identity. We dictate the contents of all physical spaces, whether this means changing a space into a fabricated place or leaving a space as a natural part of the world.

The evidence of physical influence on our physical, social and psychological health is present within our homes and workspaces. Researchers have long reported the impact wrought by every aspect of the environment, from lighting, temperature, furnishings and colour to the messages we choose to display on our walls.

Our physical environments shape us, just as they are shaped by us. The mythologist and author Joseph Campbell suggested that the height of the buildings in any town or city sends inhabitants a clear message about the hierarchy of governance; where church and cathedral spires once stood out among the rooftops, now it is often banks or other corporations which dominate the skyline. Advertising and marketing billboards vie for prime position to influence our preferences and purchases.

Turning Back Time

One of the most fascinating experiments exploring the impact of our context is Professor Ellen Langer's 1979 'Counterclockwise experiment'. Professor Langer is one of the world's most influential social psychologists. Her work has increased awareness and understanding of the power of context in many settings including in our hospitals and in nature. Her Counterclockwise study is arguably her most famous work. Langer conducted this experiment to explore the impact of social context on biological age. Eight men in their late seventies were invited to stay in a '1950s' holiday home for a week. The home, a converted monastery in New Hampshire, US, had been meticulously decorated with a 1950s theme. Everything in the building was representative of 1959, including the newspapers, the furnishings, the pictures on the walls and the activities on offer.

The eight men were invited to step back twenty years in time for a week, and to act as if it were indeed 1959. For example, they were asked to talk about 1950s news events in the present tense, invited to watch a movie from 1959 as if it were a new release and to listen to a 1950s sports match on the radio as if it were happening in real time.

In addition, the subjects were treated by staff as if they were men in their fifties, not their seventies, and not requiring any special care or attention. They were told not to bring current photos and not to refer to their 1970s lives in any way.

Before the experiment commenced, the men were assessed on a range of physical and psychological measures that are known to relate significantly with biological age. They were reassessed on the same measures once the experiment was completed.

The results were astounding. All participants had significantly improved on a variety of measures of their biological age over the course of the week. Their memory and overall cognitive abilities had improved; they were stronger, more agile and had improved appetites. Some even demonstrated better eyesight. It appeared that the changes in their context – particularly their physical context – had impacted every aspect of their physical functioning. Many of the men had been walking unsteadily at the start of the experiment, but they all joined in a spontaneous game of touch football while waiting for the bus to collect them at the end of the week.

Ground-breaking though it was, Ellen Langer's 'Counterclockwise' study should be viewed with caution. It was based on only a small sample size and I have found no evidence of a longer-term follow-up with the men, or of the study being replicated. Even so, the experiment gives us a significant example of the power of social context, including our physical surroundings, over every aspect of our health and wellbeing.

I wonder if you have ever had the opportunity to attend a reunion that has enabled you to rekindle a younger version of yourself? Or even simply heard an old song on the radio, smelled a change in the weather, or come across an old treasured possession and been compelled to change your world, if just for a moment, to revisit yourself from times past?

Ultimately, wellbeing means mindfully and consciously connecting with physical 'spaces' so that they become physical 'places' with attributed positive meaning and purpose.

In summary, the contextual wellbeing framework recognises people as socially constructed beings, whose social identities reach far beyond the boundaries of the physical bodies they are in.

We are not simply individuals or even members of groups, living in isolation of the broader human reality of our world. We are social beings created by and creating the social contexts in which we are from, and to which we contribute. The four pillars of social context: relationships with others, human-made rules, internalised norms and the physical spaces around us, intertwine to create our shared experience of ourselves, our reality and our 'life' as people.

We are born as humans, we continually become people.

NINE

Strong Goals Held Loosely

OUR SOCIAL IDENTITY CAN appear fairly fixed and permanent when the contexts of our lives remain consistent and predictable day to day. In contrast, changes in our social identity and social behaviour occur when we change our context or our connections within them.

Socially constructed aspects of our personality ebb and flow with the changing tides of place and time. Our plans, ideas and wishes grow, move and shift as we grow up, mature and grow older. Our emotions rise and fall as we react to the gains and losses of life, the making and breaking of our past, present and even our imagined connections. For example, time spent performing songs and dance routines to an enthusiastic parent when we are young, may encourage us to develop creativity, confidence and self-expression. If, however, we then repeatedly fail to make the cut for the school play despite our best efforts to be selected, we may develop reserve, self-doubt and caution. But if we then leave school and join a drama group, we may once again find our more expressive and assured self through performance. In contrast, a child may come across as quiet and shy if brought up with the influence of quiet and shy parents; but find their inner extrovert bursting out when they become part of an outspoken group of friends. We may feel life is wonderful at the start of a new relationship, but the same life may feel exhausting if that relationship falters or dies. In contrast, we may feel life is dull and exhausting at a school where we struggle to find friends, but once we find 'our tribe' at university we learn to see both the world and ourselves through a more supportive lens.

We find our 'best life' in the balance between our current context and our innermost sense of who we want to be. When we lead our best life – a life of wellbeing – we experience engagement and belonging. We experience belonging by *connecting* with our social context with authenticity, openness and congruence with our inner voice.

We experience engagement when we act within our context according to our deepest sense of who we are and how we most want to experience life: i.e. our values.

Let's now explore the importance of values – first, in understanding ourselves as people, and second, in relation to our goals, aims and ideals.

The Things that Matter

Values are ways of being and behaving that are important to the very core of who we are and how we want to experience life. For example, I can confidently state that 'compassion, equity and family' are particularly important values for me. Being compassionate, standing up for equity and creating a cohesive family unit all matter to me, every moment of every day. I will put aside my social anxiety to talk controversially about the need to be less competitive and more equitable in schools. I will challenge someone taunting an animal or child, even though I hate confrontation. I will sit up until midnight with a distressed child, insist on family dinnertime every day and turn down offers of work if work means taking too much time away from those I love most. Compassion, equity and family all really matter to me. I can say with confidence that they are at the heart of my strongest values. This may also be true for you. We often share the same values as others in our cultures and communities.

Values are the things in life that we resonate with, which have congruence with our core identity and our earliest development as a social being. They form the basis of many of our strongest beliefs about what is important in the world, about where we want to go in life, and about what attitudes and behaviours we choose to adopt.

We are not defined by our values. Our values are not 'us'. But they are powerful drivers of our life, influencing our choices, aims and ideals.

If you want to identify your values, consider a time when you felt truly connected to someone else's actions. What was the situation? What attitudes and behaviours were resonating with you? What made the *experience* a meaningful one? What touched you emotionally? For example, when she was twelve, my youngest daughter Tess once told me that she had left an online chat because the others in it had deliberately excluded one of her friends. Tess stood up for her belief in inclusion, at the risk of upsetting her friends and possibly alienating herself from them. The courage she showed in doing so made me proud because having the courage of your convictions is a value I hold dear. If your child told you the same story, it may resonate with you because you liked the fact your child was being kind, or because she was making an independent choice. Identifying both 'what' and 'why' something matters, can help us to understand our values more clearly.

If you can't think of a recent experience, it can also be interesting to consider recent movies you have watched or a book you have read where you have felt connected to the actions of a character. If we experience a story that moves us, the story undoubtedly resonates with a value we hold dear.

Alternatively, it can be helpful to ask yourself one or more of the following questions, as a way to access your values, and distinguish them from specific goals:

- How do you want to *experience* life? (As opposed to what do you want to achieve in life?)

- If you had all the money and status you could imagine, how would you spend your time?
- How do you want to be remembered by the people you love?

When we understand our values, we better understand how to connect with our world in a way that honours our core identity, how to set useful goals, and indeed, what goals to set next. Similarly, understanding of others' values helps us understand more about them and the goals they set. Our values develop within the very first experiences we have in life. This means they are foundational in defining who we are as a person, and what matters to us throughout our life. As with all of our socially created layers, they can change and develop as we move through life. They are, however, generally fairly constant throughout our life, whether we live by them or not. This is simply because they are the first layers of our social self upon which all else is built.

If you want to understand what your values are, then you need to understand *how* you want to do something, far more than you need to understand *what* you want to achieve. For example, consider why you might go for a walk on the beach on a sunny day. You could think of your answer in terms of your goals (the whats). For example, 'I want to walk five kilometres, get to the edge of the water and back, lose weight or spot a dolphin.' Alternatively, you could consider your answer in terms of your desired experience (the how). For example, 'I want to *experience* nature, spend time outdoors, participate in exercise.'

Value driven experiences drive us; they are about doing and being. In contrast, goals pull us; they are about outcomes and achieving.

Risk, Probability and Consequence

In early 2021, I listened to a conversation between sports psychologist Dr Michael Gervais and world-renowned rock climber Alex Honnold on Gervais' *Finding Mastery* podcast. I say 'world renowned', but in truth, I had not heard of Honnold and his awe-inspiring adventures until a few months previously when I had watched the Oscar-winning documentary *Free Solo* in the midst of the pandemic lockdown. I am now very aware that Alex Honnold is a climber who has become widely known for his 'free solo' ascents of various enormous hillsides and mountains around the world.

Free climbing means to climb under only your own power. You do not use any special equipment, except climbing shoes, to help yourself move upward. For example, you do not pull on bolts or ropes or use makeshift ladders. Most styles of 'free climbing' do, however, use some sort of protection to prevent the climber from falling. For example, the climber is often attached by a rope to the rockface, another climber, or the top of a climb. The equipment keeps the climber safe but does not directly help them to climb.

To climb something 'solo' means to do so alone – and using no protection whatsoever from falling.. The adventurer climbs without safety ropes, and without being attached to the wall, the mountain, or to another climber.

Alex Honnold combined both forms of climbing – free climbing and solo climbing – so his incredible pursuits are known as 'free solo' climbing. A 'free solo' climb is one in which the climber is both climbing 'freely' – without any manufactured aids to help them (other than shoes and a chalk bag) – and climbing 'solo' with no protection from falls. Many people will likely be more familiar with the efforts of the mischievous French climber Alain Robert, known the world over as the 'Human Spider-Man' for his breathtaking (but not necessarily legal) 'free solo' scalings of tall urban buildings and skyscrapers – using only climbing shoes and chalk, with no safety devices at all.

Alex Honnold shot to stardom when he featured in the *Free Solo* documentary. The documentary, filmed over more than two years, follows Honnold's journey to prepare for and finally achieve a free solo ascent of the imposing El Capitan granite wall in Yosemite National Park. El Capitan's vertical granite wall soars more than 3000 feet from bottom to top.

Sixty years ago, American 'big wall' climber Warren Harding and his team were the first people to scale the El Capitan wall. They took 45 days to reach the summit. By 2020, most experienced climbers were taking four to six days to conquer this incredible rock face. These experienced climbers often camp on the wall in between days of climbing, in a secure 'portaledge': A type of hammock with a hard base that is secured to the wall. They generally climb with the help of ropes, climbing aids, protection and the assurance that if they fall, they will, almost certainly, be fine.

As far as I am aware, as I write this, there are only three professional climbers who have managed to free climb El Capitan in one day. This is an exceptional feat. Someone like me, who is a middle-aged non-climber, would probably not make the first three feet up the wall.

In 2017, Alex Honnold managed to completely free solo El Capitan in just three hours and fifty-six minutes.

This feat is remarkable in so many ways.

Probability vs Consequence

First, the physical requirements to climb such a tall and sheer rock face are astounding. To put its towering scale into context, El Capitan is two-and-a-half times as tall as the Empire State Building and more than three times as high as the Eiffel Tower. At 2,716 feet, the Burj Khalifa in Dubai is the world's tallest building, but it is still shorter than El Capitan. To be fit enough to climb something this high, this sheer, and this uncompromising – and to do it in under four hours – took an incredible amount of dedication, determination and discipline. All leading to an incredible amount of climbing skill, physical strength, flexibility and stamina.

Moreover, Alex Honnold's accomplishment is remarkable from a psychological point of view. For just about the entire climb, (i.e. other than the first few feet), the consequences of slipping without safety precautions in place are catastrophic. A fall from one missed tiny foothold or one lost precarious handhold would lead to certain death. Yet Honnold remained calm, centred and focused the entire way to the top.

Most people with a healthy respect of fear would never actively choose to face such perceived danger, even if they believed they had the necessary physical skills and strengths to achieve success. The impact of unbridled adrenaline and unabashed fear would have most of us quaking at just 30 feet up. We would certainly not be focused, calm and confident poised precariously at thousands of feet above the ground. Yet there Honnold was. At one instant, he was holding on with just one foot on one hold, his hands flat on the glassy wall, and that one hold was less than the width of a pencil. Yet, there he was: calm, focused and confident.

I am sure some people would suggest that Honnold is pretty damn crazy to attempt something so inarguably dangerous. Others may consider him unequivocally brave and courageous, both for the climb and for the determined pursuit of his dreams.

Alex Honnold suggests that his climb was not overly dangerous, nor was he at great risk. Rather he was simply taking the next step in his journey to be the best climber he could be. Honnold believes that *we need to distinguish between risk and consequence*. He was so completely prepared for the climb he believed the risk to be minimal. Thus, despite the terrible consequences of failure, he believes his choice was not a dangerous or foolhardy one. Rather, Honnold has been known to ponder on the vast numbers of people who take deadly long-term risks by eating poorly, surviving on minimum exercise or abusing substances, every day.

Honnold's philosophy raises an interesting idea. It suggests that, to ensure we attain success in life, we need to focus our time and efforts on risk minimisation and self-betterment, rather than on the consequences of failure, or indeed a longing for success. With this message, he encourages us to shift our focus from outcomes to process.

Process vs Outcomes

Both risk reduction and ongoing self-improvement involve a steady focus on process. In contrast, continued attention paid to the consequences of failure or success, involves a focus on outcomes. My own research into goal setting and motivation in the 1990s repeatedly found that individuals who focus on process – rather than outcomes – are ultimately more successful in attaining their goals. They minimise the risk of failure by engaging in their progress and on attaining proficiency. I have also found that process-focused people of all ages are happier and more content with life than are those focused on outcomes. If we focus on the process of pursuing our goal—say, for example, learning the material in our doctoral program well rather than simply obtaining the degree – any increase in competency feels like success. If we invest in the journey, we feel a greater sense of connection and autonomy on that journey whatever the outcome may be. We find flow in our activities and we are more likely to thrive and find the best in ourselves. In contrast, if we focus on potential outcomes – good or bad – we are less likely to connect with the day-to-day journey of our lives. We are less likely to feel a sense of growing competency if we don't reach our goals, and we are less likely to feel we have ownership and agency over the things we do.

To further epitomise the importance of a focus on process, Alex Honnold states that he decided the time was right to climb El Capitan free solo, when all of his preparation was done, e.g. his physical and mental training, clearing the rock face of loose stones and anticipating good weather. He needed to have many factors in place, rather than have a particular date and time set as a deadline, as a timetabled event.

This subtle shift in thinking strongly suggests that Honnold remained focused on the journey all the way to the climb. The climb became his inevitable next step rather than the pinnacle of his hard work and determination.

In the podcast where I first learned about Honnold, Dr Michael Gervais asked him how he sets his goals in life. Honnold replied by saying he sets '*strong goals, held loosely*'. He goes on to explain that, as an example, he sets very definite, deliberate goals at the start of the Yosemite climbing season. However, he is happy to achieve only some of them. He is happy to change both direction and focus as his context – his physical and mental experiences, life events, energy levels, interest – ebbs and flows. Ultimately, if he feels he is learning, adventuring and growing, he feels a sense of achievement and wellbeing.

Road Signs vs Destination Markers

With this simple, eloquent statement – strong goals, held loosely – Honnold lets us know that he chooses to direct his life according to his core values, rather than according to any particular outcome. He appears to deeply value a pathway that is authentic and feels continually progressive. For this young athlete, climbing El Capitan was, indeed, simply the next step in a life of adventure, growth and engagement.

There is so much we can learn from someone like Alex Honnold. His dedication, determination, and more importantly his calm, centred and confident approach to life, speak volumes to the importance of staying focused on the values that drive us. Honnold reminds us that it is important to work towards our goals but that we are driven by our values and by the bigger experience of our lives rather than focused solely on achieving any particular goals. He reminds us to work to reduce risk as we learn and grow, and to commit to the experience of living more than to any particular outcome or achievement.

If we are willing to be driven by our core values, and see our goals as signposts, rather than destination markers measuring our success, we can keep our eyes on what really matters. We can ensure we are driven by our values, not pulled by our goals. We can thrive, no matter what challenges we face.

When setting your goals for the future, remember to ask, 'What *experience* matters to me in this context' before asking 'What do I want to attain'. For example, before putting in that offer on a potential new home, in addition to asking if your move represents reaching a goal, ask yourself if this home offers you a chance to live life more fully according to what matters. Is it close to treasured friends and family, or does it have the potential to be part of a community? Is it close to nature or shared facilities or perhaps a local cafe? Does it promote shared space or segregated space? Does it represent comfort or hard work? Is it animal friendly? Grandparent friendly? Is it the right place to welcome a child? You may not want or need to ask all of these questions, and they may not all matter. However, some of them might resonate with your values, and then they become important to explore.

Live life according to your values and you will connect to the life that you lead, and those who share it with you.

If you want to live according to your values, be sure to set strong goals, held loosely.

TEN

Letting go of Competition

IT IS VERY HARD to meaningfully connect with other people if you see them as barriers to your own life success. Yet, it seems that, at least in the materialist world, we encourage our children to consider success as a comparative process from the moment they are born. We don't simply encourage them to consider success as achieving their goals. We also encourage them to consider success as achieving their goals *more* quickly and more effectively than others. As such we encourage our children, and indeed ourselves, to consider success in comparison to the 'stuff', status and power that we see others attain.

Does Competition Equal Success?

Before you think that this is not true of you, be aware that this process does not necessarily happen with too much conscious planning or control. It is not so much that we are shouting for our kids to be better, brighter or more acknowledged than their friends. Rather, we subtly but relentlessly encourage them to outshine their peers, often without really realising we are doing it. We encourage our children to enter the sports carnival, the debating team, the dance competition. We sing their praises if they appear to be speaking/crawling/running/doing advanced maths ahead of the 'average' person their age. We whoop with delight when they win an award in assembly even though we pretend winning is not important when they lose.

It is not that we want our children to be better than everyone else's: rather it is that we want them to have every opportunity for success. And all too often, we understand success to be a measure of our accomplishments compared with our peers.

The Impact of Relentless Competition

In the previous chapter, I suggested that we would all benefit from redefining success according to our ability to live by our values rather than our ability to achieve any particular goal. As such, a well-led life becomes a life in which we continually strive to know and accept ourselves, to connect meaningfully and authentically within our social contexts, and to live according to our values. If we can truly understand success in these terms, competition becomes a meaningless ploy. Unlike quantifiable measures of success such as grade outcomes, money or fame; authenticity, self-determination and living a connected life are things that are not easily boxed and quantified with any real meaning. Rather, our measures of these more personal and social aspects of living are in the way they make us *experience* life. If we feel well, and are living life according to our values, then we can consider ourselves to be successful, no matter what we achieve, or how anyone else is faring.

Sadly, if we insist on concrete, external measures of progress assessed in relation to others; we may end up feeling threatened by others' achievements. Similarly, we may perceive ourselves to have failed if we do not stack up against the material and concrete accomplishments of others.

This means that everyone, at some level, is as much our competition as they may also be essentially our allies. As we are all only too aware, competition leads to detachment, jealousy, resentment and threat; none of which are sound pillars for making deep connections.

I see competition seeping into any group that starts to covet money, status or power. Even in the halls of wellbeing science, there are increasing numbers of people who began their professional journey interested in understanding and helping others but who then often fall prey to competing with their colleagues for more dubious measures of success. We all want to pay the mortgage, put food on the table and possibly place the occasional bottle of wine in the fridge, but in my many years of experience organising wellbeing conferences, I have found that those who seek the most recognition and the biggest pay cheque appear to be the least content.

It can be useful to ask yourself from time to time whether you are truly pleased for others' accomplishments in life or whether you feel threatened or inexplicably upset by them. When our neighbour's new car, our colleague's promotion, or our best friend's new romance make us feel uneasy more than pleased, then perhaps it is time to examine our own measures of success.

It is also worth considering that, for many of us, the way *others* measure success matters to us just as much as how we measure success for ourselves. It can be easy to wonder if inner confidence and a self-determined life are little match against a lack of comparative status and wealth. Could the cost of investing in spiritual awareness, rather than material gain, be loneliness and a life of exclusion?

Hopefully not in the slightest.

The more we establish our inner whole-being, the greater our capacity to achieve in all areas of life, and that includes connecting with others in a meaningful way. As such, the only exclusion that self-development brings, is exclusion from groups to which we never belonged in the first place.

At some deep core level, we all know that a meaningful life stems from our ability to authentically connect and live with integrity and self-respect. As such, we are naturally drawn to the confidence, kindness and compassion of spiritually aware others. When a person who knows themselves well enters the room, we often navigate towards them. We want them to like us, and we can't help but like them. Consider the elusive quality of charisma. Although we often consider charismatic people to possess a mysterious inner quality, they are more likely to display a mix of self-acceptance, self-confidence and social skills. As such, charisma and long-term attractiveness are not about physical appearance per se, nor are they direct reflections of status or material wealth.

Your ongoing wellbeing is, in part, dependent upon your measures of success. If you choose measures that incite continuous competition with others, it is harder to deeply connect within your social groups and harder to master the art of resilience when things go wrong. It is also harder to feel in control of your success because it is so dependent on others' performance, which is largely out of your control.

Let us ensure that our sense of success is more about our personal development than it is about any social competition for recognition, status or material gains. Far better that we cherish our relationships without competition and constant downward or upwards comparisons. Far better for our sense of competency, our feelings of ownership and autonomy and our relationships; far better for our wellbeing and resilience.

Our experience of success is more dependent on how we *define* success than on *what* we achieve.

ELEVEN

A Self-Determined Life

LIVING AUTHENTICALLY, ACCORDING TO our values, helps us to experience both *engagement* and *belonging*.

When we experience belonging and engagement in life, instead of just being physically present, we internalise the social norms of our context in a way that resonates with our inner voice, all the way through our socially constructed sense of self. Life makes sense because the social and cultural things we do match who and 'how' we want to be. They represent 'just the way life is', and indeed 'just the way we are', in ways that support us authentically and meaningfully. This kind of support ensures that we have met our key needs for authentic connections with others, engagement in the things we do, and a sense of autonomy in our daily lives across all four domains of every social context in which we find ourselves.

Society's Unwritten Rules

The social norms we internalise are not necessarily rational, nor are they open to question. Rather they are the unwritten rules that guide us and create a sense of 'how the world is'. For example, in western society, at least prior to the pandemic, most of us rarely questioned whether shaking hands was an odd way to greet someone; it is just what we would do.

Similarly, we don't think it strange to have sweet dessert after a savoury course, it is just what we do. We don't question why we love dogs but eat cows, why we wear a bikini at the beach but would never walk the streets in our underwear, why we bury our dead with music, dress our babies in pink or blue depending on their birth sex, or why we have roast dinner on Sundays. It is just what we do.

In contrast, when we feel like an outsider, the norms we see around us make far less sense. When we are on the outside of a group, or feel uncomfortable and unconnected within one, we have a very different perspective to the group members who experience belonging.

When I was living in the Guildford student subculture of the 1980s, I was most definitely an outsider from mainstream society. At that time, my life consisted of an immersion in a world of rock music from the 1960s and 1970s (I think I had albums from every singer and group who played at Woodstock). It was a world frequently filled with smokey hedonism, late-night conversation, coloured hair and Greenpeace memberships. A world in which I made and embraced some of the best friendships I have ever had; but also one in which I frequently felt 'a bit out of place'. My growing desire to become more integrated into mainstream life was continually challenged by my reluctance to accept many mainstream norms. I would constantly ask: 'Why is it OK to treat some animals so badly, like the ones bred for food, or the wild foxes that live in the countryside?' 'Why is it attractive for women to paint their faces, but for men to appear without enhancement or disguise?' 'Why is it deemed "better" by so many people to be white rather than black?' 'Straight but not gay?' 'Why do men in suits command more respect than men in working clothes?' 'Why is it considered attractive for women to wear shoes that cripple their backs and prevent them from running?'

I continually questioned the value and the logic of mainstream social norms that were never meant to represent reason, nor created with equity in mind. I was questioning the irrational norms of the groups to which I did *not* belong.

Have you ever visited another country or lived in another culture? If so, were there customs that struck you as odd or strange, despite being 'just the way life is' to those immersed in that way of life? Or have you ever welcomed someone from a different culture to your own? If so, did you notice that they questioned things you have never thought about, such as how it's customary to say hello, the way your culture approaches mealtimes, or the way you dress?

When we feel like an outsider in a community, we can find it hard to see the logic in the most basic of social behaviours. In contrast, when we experience a genuine sense of belonging, we internalise the norms of our communities and normative behaviour is no longer a choice. Consider a fish tank full of vibrant tropical fish. We notice the colours and idiosyncrasies of the fish, the pebbles and the underwater plants but we barely notice the water that is essential to the structure and survival of the fish world. When we have internalised the norms of our communities, they become like the water in the tank: vital to sustain consistency and to keep us connected, but barely noticeable in our day-to-day observations.

Creating a social identity that supports our inner voice, our values and our goals helps us to experience optimum wellbeing when the circle of our identity is rising from the spring to the summer. It also means we will be stronger and more resilient when we inevitably head into the winter, and resilience is required.

The Three Key Human Needs of Wellbeing

The meaningful connections we form within all four domains of every social context are at their best when they support our experience of being and acting as a meaningful connected member of the social worlds to which we belong. As such, healthy connections meet our key needs for authentic, accepting relationships, engagement in the things we do and a sense of autonomy and ownership over our life. These three key needs have repeatedly been found to be essential for the development of our self-determination and autonomous motivation as well as for our overall wellbeing. In fact, they form the basis of Professor Richard Ryan and Edward Deci's world-renowned Self-Determination Theory which describes these needs as relatedness (connection to others), competency (engagement) and autonomy.

In the mid-1980s, professors Deci and Ryan wrote a book titled 'Self-Determination and Intrinsic Motivation in Human Behavior' in which Self-Determination Theory (SDT) was formally introduced and established as a world-leading theory of motivation and self-actualisation. Since the 2000s, research exploring and expanding SDT has increased significantly, and the theory has also become prominent in modern ideas about wellbeing.

The theory suggests that these three needs – relatedness, competency and autonomy – are essential to self-motivation and self-determination in life. I believe that experiencing a self-determined and autonomously motivated life is akin to experiencing 'wellbeing in action'. SDT has repeatedly identified these three needs as predictive of improved wellbeing in all kinds of people from across many cultures around the world.

The Limits of Behavioural Approaches to Social Development

My psychiatric nurse training in the mid-1980s taught me much about the importance of connecting to a context that meets our key needs as well as the dangers of losing autonomy.

Many of the patients living in psychiatric hospitals at that time had been resident for 20+ years. These patients were generally heavily drugged and highly institutionalised. This means they had lost their ability to make choices and behave in a self-determined autonomous way. For many of them, even deciding which pair of socks to put on in the morning had become an unmanageable choice. Leading analysts such as Freud had certainly made their mark on psychotherapy for the 'worried well' and those experiencing short hospital stays; but psychiatrists in the 1980s rarely viewed psychotherapy as appropriate for the thousands of people living fairly permanently in psychiatric wards around the UK.

So, instead of learning to use effective communication skills, psychiatric nurses learned about token economies and behavioural compliance. We were encouraged to use rewards to elicit 'good behaviours', and punishment (or the withdrawal of rewards) to stop unwanted ones. Long-stay patients were literally 'paid to behave' with tokens which they could swap for cigarettes, soft drinks or sweets.

These core behavioural techniques I was taught reflected the state of academic psychology at that time, which favoured behavioural approaches to understanding the human condition. In fact, many of the behavioural approaches of the time had been influenced by animal training. Think Pavlov and conditioned responses. Certainly, I use rewards to get my dog Barney to be compliant and it works well. Humans, however, are very different from dogs .

There was little understanding of the fact that, unlike most animal behaviour, human behaviour is driven by complex thought processes, built upon complex beliefs, attitudes and values. Moreover, the superior cognitive abilities of humans over that of other animal species results in a basic requirement for self-determination as well as for community. Unlike most other social animals, we are not content to live in an unquestioned hierarchy as members of the pack. More than any other animal, we need a large degree of autonomy in our lives, to have a daily sense of choice and control, and to feel valued as unique beings making unique contributions to the world.

Looking back at my student nurse days, it seems crazy that we were trying to bribe long-stay patients to 'behave' with cigarettes and candy rather than trying to help them to become self-determined citizens through kindness, care and regular psychotherapy.

It also seems crazy that the extreme lack of autonomy afforded to patients actually served to create so many of their long-term difficulties.

Ironically, most long-stay patients I met in the 1980s remained in hospital because they had such crippling levels of institutionalisation, rather than any other psychological illness.

When our autonomy is not supported, we crumble.

Among the long-stay patients I cared for were Polish immigrants who had come to the UK during World War II as young men and who were put into psychiatric hospitals simply because they could not speak English. I cared for elderly women who had become pregnant as teenagers, out of marriage, and had been quickly removed from public family life and the possibilities of public humiliation and shame.

I met so many people whose only crime had been to be living in the wrong place at the wrong time. How easy it is to make someone an outsider simply because they do not fit the system.

After twenty or thirty years in care, these people could not decide between tea or coffee (not that anyone would want the chicory infused instant coffee of 1980s England). Nor could these institutionalised people cope with the idea of a more self-determined existence, as seen in the dismal failure of the late 1980s attempt to re-establish long-stay patients into local community life.

These innocent outsiders had become casualties of a system that did not understand the importance of trying to meet patients' needs, but which instead put stock in trying to garner their compliance.

Despite my desire to offer something more helpful to patients than drugs and rewards, I was young, nervous and completely lacking in any skills to form meaningful relationships with people with these levels of communication difficulties.

One More Cigarette for Sam

My first placement was on a male long-stay ward. A collection of rooms over two floors, separated by clanging corridors and locked doors, deep in the middle of the old psychiatric hospital. Some of the rooms still had radiators installed out of reach on the ceiling, to ensure that 'out of control' patients were not able to hurt themselves when locked inside.

I had one patient who I will call Sam.

Sam was in his forties when I met him and had been living in the mental hospital for 25 years. He was over-medicated to the point of a constant tremor, slurred speech and regular seizures, and was lacking in any ability to deal with anything outside of a very rigid routine.

I was warned to make sure his knife and fork were placed precisely next to his plate at dinner time. Otherwise, I was told, he might become violent.

Not a good beginning to my relationship with Sam, or with the nursing process.

Still I persevered.

Then after just two weeks of my placement, I was left temporarily alone as the only staff member on the ward, which by default put me 'in charge'. An illegal move, but the mental health service was very under-resourced then, as it is now.

I was given several packets of Benson and Hedges cigarettes and was instructed to let Sam have one cigarette every twenty minutes. I was further informed that if he was given more, he would become overly agitated and possibly aggressive.

After just five minutes of my being the lone staff member on the ward, Sam came up to me and demanded a cigarette. I nervously reached up to give him one and light it. Despite being overly medicated, Sam still stood at six feet four inches and was an imposing presence. In contrast, I am five foot four.

Sam walked slowly away with his lit cigarette hanging from his mouth. After only five minutes more, he came back and asked for another. I nervously said: 'Sorry Sam, no, not for another fifteen minutes.'

The next thing I knew, I was waking up with a bleeding nose and a very sore head.

Two other patients came to my rescue and started screaming. The resulting commotion eventually meant a nurse arrived to help. I was to end up with a severe headache. The force of Sam's punch had thrown me heavily against the wall. My nose was thankfully not broken but I would be living with two black eyes for a while.

I took a day off work to recover, but not before I was instructed to give Sam an injection of Largactil, a sedating antipsychotic drug, 'to show him I was in charge'.

The next time I was on duty, Sam tried to strangle me. Fortunately for me, a competent, qualified male nurse was close by this time, and swiftly pulled his hands from around my throat.

The next week, Sam managed to lift and throw a half-full urn of boiling water at me. It narrowly missed.

I was terrified of Sam.

It took me years to realise he was probably even more terrified of me.

The Cost of Extrinsic Rewards

It is of little surprise to know that token economies – the use of rewards to encourage desired behaviours – are now rarely employed in mental health facilities. You may, however, be surprised to know that they form the model for most of the reward systems still used in large institutions around the developed world where gaining compliance is seen as important. Most noticeably, reward systems are pervasive in prisons and schools. In our schools, we may not pay children cigarettes to get them to refrain from attacking us, but we certainly have learned to pay them in gel pens to keep them sitting still at their desks.

The use of extrinsic rewards can indeed achieve a certain level of compliance. But at what cost?

Their use leads to a gradual diminishing of people's ability to be self-determined and make good choices, when no one is watching, or when the situation demands creativity and flexibility. As much as I want my dog to be consistently compliant, I hope that my children will one day leave home as self-determined people who make good choices even when no one is watching. When we have our key needs for autonomy, relationships and competency met, we feel 'whole', as social beings and as individuals.

In fact, the irony of being an 'individual' is that it requires healthy connections to 'other people' to exist as a concept or, indeed, as an experience.

When we have wellbeing, we feel seen and heard by the social world in which we exist, and by which we define ourselves, and this means we experience a sense of our own value and our own voice. When we have voice and value, we experience life with meaning and purpose.

Being and Doing

My 2018 book *Contextual Wellbeing: Creating Positive Schools from the Inside Out* defines and explores wellbeing in schools. The book encourages educators and parents to consider wellbeing as a social phenomenon, rather than purely as an individual state. It is based on my firm belief that wellbeing is an interplay between our best individual self and our best environment. As such, happiness and success are far more than individual pursuits, or even individual responsibilities. The ongoing creation of healthy connections to others and to the world around us contributes to a healthy sense of our whole-being, which gives us an experience of wellbeing in the everchanging cycle of our life.

I wrote *Contextual Wellbeing* as a call to challenge and change our understanding of wellbeing and resilience in schools. I want to encourage schools to stop holding each child completely responsible for their individual wellbeing, and to instead understand that the school system plays an important role in supporting the needs, and consequently the wellbeing, of all members of the community. We need to ask not 'What is wrong' with a troubled child, but rather, 'How can we better support a troubled child's needs?'

Moreover, I wrote the book as a wake-up call to increase equity in our schools. It is vital that we support the development of belonging, creativity, psychological safety and voice for *all* young people, not just those who fit the system well. We need to ensure that everyone can experience growth and a sense of success that is independent of the growth and success of others. As such, we need to put aside ideas of success being a zero-sum game and focus on building collaborative school communities, rather than continually competitive ones.

I wrote *Contextual Wellbeing* to help young people in schools; however, it is important to be aware that the concepts I explore in that book apply to *every* context in which we find ourselves, as children and as adults. When life is good, in *any* given context, we experience wellbeing through the meaningful connections we form. These connections are built through our 'being' part of a context and through our actions within it. As such, wellbeing is both about 'being' and about 'doing'. When we build connections through our being and our doing, we become part of a life that is bigger than we are.

This ultimately means the impermanence of our individual life is far easier to bear.

In fact, the key reason it is so important for us all to contribute to our communities is because we all face the certainty of our own impermanence, our own death. If we can become a meaningful part of a community, then we can better deal with the inevitability of our dying. As the community lives on, so too does the impact we had upon it.

In *Contextual Wellbeing* I used Mexico's Day of the Dead to illustrate the social essence of our identity. This is an important annual day for people to remember and celebrate the lives of those they have loved and lost. The Mexican community shares a belief that death comes in three stages. First, we experience physical death; second, we are buried; and third, we are forgotten. It is only when we are forgotten that we are truly considered to be dead. This understanding of death emphasises the importance of our identity beyond our physical form.

We reside in every aspect of the context in which we live and die. Just as the boundaries of our physical form define us, so we are defined by the space around us.

In Living Memories

Consider someone you have loved who is no longer in your life. Beyond photos and messages, how do you hold onto them in your environment? I have a scarf that belonged to my father that I keep sacred and safe. It still smells of him, or at least of the laundry detergent my mother used.

I also have a glass paperweight that belonged to my maternal grandparents. I used to play with it when I visited them as a child. It represents my happiest times staying with them.

And then there is the flint... a brittle, hard stone found in the Norfolk countryside and as a building block of many Norfolk houses and churches. Over time, my family and I have collected a pile of flint pieces which now sits in a glass vase in my living room.

As my friend Lorna knows, the people we love the most live on in us even when they are no longer physically around. Lorna and her mother, who is now in her early nineties, are both passionate artists. They enjoy a close, creative and caring relationship. Lorna talks to her mum about all things, and still seeks her advice on important decisions and dilemmas.

Lorna told me that she had once said to her mum: 'I don't know what I am going to do when you are gone. What will I do when I need to ask you a question?'

Her mother had answered: 'You will still ask me questions.' She then smiled, paused and added: 'And you will still hear my replies.'

When you love someone deeply enough, they are with you, even when they are not.

TWELVE

Holding onto Yourself in a World of Constant Change

THE HAPPIEST MEMORIES OF my childhood are of family caravanning holidays. At some magical point in just about every summer of the 1970s, the day would arrive when we all piled into the car and headed up the drive with the caravan trundling behind us, and with much excitement and glee. I would sit in the back of the Volvo with my two brothers. My dad would be driving, and my mum would be sitting with the dog and a pile of paper maps on her knee. We occasionally also took the cat which was squeezed onto the back seat with us children.

The caravan was securely fastened to the car's tow bar.

Each year we headed to a different part of the UK to climb hills, stand in echoing cathedrals and eat our body weight in fish and chips in small country towns. I found the cathedrals all pretty dull, although I was always amused at my cheery parents' enthusiasm for every stained-glass window and marble altar. I found climbing hills strenuous, and it was hard to appreciate the joy of a view. Views are for adults far more than for children. Yet, I still loved these holidays, every day, from dawn to dusk.

We travelled from campsite to campsite, often staying one or two nights at each. Every new stop seemed like an exciting adventure, whether it was a fully serviced site with showers on tap, or a muddy field with nothing but a few cows to add to the scenery.

I vividly remember the smell of the gas stove, the excitement of turning the small couches into small beds, and playing endless games of rummy and blackjack, with buttons for child-friendly betting. We each had a small cupboard for our things, and it was always exciting to fill mine, which I mainly did with stuffed toys, art materials and a few clothes jammed in on top.

Most vividly of all, I remember feeling safe and secure as a family on holiday. I loved that we were all in such close proximity to each other and all had the luxury of time to be present. I loved exploring and playing and meeting new people. I loved the ice creams and the hot chips and all the other snacks in between.

My parents must have spent countless hours preparing before we left each year. I remember the excitement of my mother filling the food storage boxes with supplies. We needed to eat instant meals that could be prepared on a two-burner camp stove and could feed five hungry mouths, and, of course, the pets. So, Mum packed lots of cans of Irish stew and hearty soup, along with canned, steamed puddings which she would serve up with canned custard. It was bliss.

In our 'normal' world, we always ate fresh home-cooked meals with plenty of home-grown salads and vegetables. Barely a can was ever seen or opened. We ate eggs from our own chickens, homemade bread and homemade jam. The concept of pudding from a can while caravanning, complete with lots of custard, seemed like heaven.

Even as I became older and started to grow beyond those magical years between learning to walk and discovering adolescence, I still loved the idea of steamed puddings in cans. No longer because they seemed like a holiday luxury, but because they had become a symbol of our being a family and having a good time. Be it small gestures or big celebratory events, family rituals and habits bond us together; deepen our wellbeing and our capacity for resilience. As Australian psychologist Andrew Fuller states, 'Family branding is important'.

Now, more than forty years later, I work to ensure that we have rituals and regular events as part of our family here in Australia. We have family dinnertime, Sunday roast and Neil and I love to watch a movie together on a Friday night.

We lack many extended family members here in Perth, but we have adopted an honorary family who help us build wellbeing with rituals small and large. My dear friend Paula has taken each of my daughters for a special meal when they reached adolescence. George always makes homemade chocolate eggs with us on Easter Sunday. We still set up Christmas stockings even though thoughts of Santa have long gone. Our friends Caroline, Jason and their son traditionally spend Boxing Day with us each year, and we share the same menu each time. And our deeply loved friend Dave arrives with a new beer for the adults in our house to sample, whenever he comes for a visit.

What treasured rituals and celebrations anchor you in your world?

It is important we do not underestimate the power of the details in the broader contexts of our lives, especially the treasured regular rituals we develop with family and friends.

THIRTEEN

The Power of Outside

ONE OF THE MOST powerful impacts of the physical spaces around us, is the impact of nature. We are born ready to interact and thrive in a natural environment. Just as we are born ready to breathe fresh air, we are born ready to appreciate all that nature can give us for our social and emotional development.

According to his 2012 report for the National Trust in the UK, naturalist Stephen Moss estimates that the outdoors area around a child's home – in which they are free to roam – has decreased by more than 90% in England since the 1970s. Moreover, he states that Britain's children watch, on average, almost two-and-a-half hours of TV per day, every single day of the year. In addition, they spend more than 20 hours a week online, mostly on social networking sites. As the children grow older, their screen time expands still further. Britain's 11–15 year olds spend an average of seven-and-a-half hours in front of a screen, every day.

The situation is similar in other developed countries. Yale University social ecology professor Stephen Kellert reported in 2015 that a typical child in the United States spent 90% of their time indoors, often on screens. In fact, children as young as two were using a screen for an average of 30 hours a week, while school aged children averaged more than 50 hours. These are alarming statistics, and I doubt they will improve in the immediate future. These same children devoted less than 30 minutes a day to free play outside in 2015, as opposed to their parents in the 1970s and 1980s, who spent four hours every day roaming outdoors.

I am not saying technology is toxic or that screen-time is the single cause of this increasingly indoor life, but these findings do suggest that the rise of home-based technology plays a significant role in 'nature deprivation'. We need to find a better balance between onscreen and outside time in young people, and indeed in ourselves.

In his 2005 book *Last Child in the Woods,* non-fiction author and journalist Richard Louv coined the term 'nature deficit disorder'. He argued that children growing up in today's world have a diminished ability to focus, to use their senses, to attend to their surroundings – in effect to be mindful – and are experiencing higher rates of physical and emotional illness. I wonder how much the rise in mental health concerns in the developed world in adults and children alike are exacerbated by our disconnect from nature, and the loss of all that nature brings us.

Stephen Moss's 2012 National Trust report suggests that this disconnection with the outdoors and the natural environment is causing physical, emotional and intellectual deficits in children's learning and development. He believes outdoor play fosters all manner of cognitive, social and emotional learning through curiosity, observation, wonder, exploration, problem-solving and creativity.

Physical health and fitness are undeniably important, but the outdoor school environment offers far more in addition to these, as Stephen Kellert observed in 2015. 'In engaging with other life from redwood trees to hedgehogs, [we] encounter an endless source of curiosity, emotional attachment and a motivation for learning. In adapting to the ever-changing, often unpredictable natural world, [we] learn to cope and problem-solve.'

Kellert's work is supported by child psychologist Aric Sigman who, in 2007, found that exposure to nature significantly boosts concentration and self-control. Sigman also identified significant improvements in mindfulness, reasoning and observational skills due to connection with the natural environment.

Spending time in nature may seem attractive to those who are thriving. However, the idea to consider getting out for some fresh air, or going for a walk in the countryside, may seem trite when we are facing the pain of severe struggle or loss. Yet, small gestures to build our connection with the natural contexts of our lives make a significant impact on our ability to live well when times are going well, and heal when times are tough.

More than Bricks and Mortar

Our identity exists in the physical space around us and our sense of autonomy is connected to our sense of choice and control of that space. Many of us will have vivid memories of the décor of our teenage bedrooms. After all, a teenager's bedroom is generally a clear expression of their emerging identity. I remember feeling 'invaded' if my mother tidied my room for me and enraged when my father suggested I remove my David Bowie posters in favour of something he regarded as more aesthetically pleasing. Our physical space matters, and having a sense of ownership over that physical space matters even more.

It is the same when it comes to our workplaces: the most effective physical environments are created when the whole community is consulted and involved in the process of change and development, from office décor to the staff room.

If we're interested in creating spaces that support our wellbeing and the wellbeing of others, it's important to think about both the direct impact of the physical environment and the indirect messages conveyed within that environment: physical space acts as a powerful voice for the other pillars of social context. In particular, it supports the creation and maintenance of the social norms and values of our family, our work and our broader community.

For example, putting your child's drawing on the fridge door says volumes about how much value you place on your child, as much as it indicates your love of their art. Similarly, the presence of family photos on your desk says family matters, even when at work.

These visual messages say volumes about the true values of the community you are in, and they can have a far bigger impact on those values than overt policy or practice. A workplace reception displaying photos of staff social events or collective projects is telling a very different story to the reception that displays the awards of high performers or a picture of the chair of the board. These publicly placed visual messages are powerful influences on culture and behaviour, and ultimately on wellbeing.

Nature matters: we are designed to thrive when we spend time in natural settings and we suffer when we are deprived of time outdoors; or we forget to invite nature indoors. In modern western society, many of us spend most if not all of our time indoors. As such, it is more important than ever that we invite nature in. Literally speaking this can be with plants and flowers (real or artificial). More figuratively, it can be with the use of natural materials depicted with a natural finish or the use of colours representing the hues and tones of nature.

We are also encouraged from birth to understand that some types of furniture represent relaxation whereas others represent work or being alert and more 'on show'. As such, it is important to reflect care and support for yourself and others with the use of physical décor and furniture that speaks of value, care and comfort. For example, carefully consider the impact of heating, lighting, airflow and the use of comfortable chairs where possible. Even on the smallest budget a throw rug and a cushion or two can transform the staffroom couch; photos of family and friends can bring life to an office, bedroom or hallway.

Implicit messages have power. *We need our walls to celebrate rather than adulate.* We need them to support equity, cohesion and community.

When we experience connection within our context with others, with the norms and rituals that define us and with the physical spaces we make into places; we have contextual wellbeing.

We are able to feel whole when we are wholly connected to the contexts of our lives.

FOURTEEN

The One About The Umbrella

Ten ladies go outside with only one umbrella between them but they don't get wet.

Why?

It isn't raining...

Connection builds our sense of belonging and ability to feel well, and live well...

...but what happens when a treasured connection is threatened or broken?

We can spend time when life is good, contemplating and preparing for life being tough.

Yet, no matter how well we attempt to prepare, it is hard to know how we will actually feel, and what we will really need, when loss and challenge comes our way.

FIFTEEN

Grief, Loss and Fractured Identities

WHEN WE EXPERIENCE LOSS or adversity, we experience threat, damage or a complete loss to one or more of the connections by which we define ourselves. For example, we might experience a lost romance or friendship. We may have to face the death of a family member or friend. We may have been given redundancy or failed to gain a longed-for promotion. We may experience the impact of illness or injury. We may move to live in a new place, like I moved to Australia, and find ourselves longing for the home we left behind. A threat or loss to one or more of our defining connections results in a fracture to our identity. We no longer feel whole; rather we feel damaged or 'lost'. We no longer 'feel ourselves'. We move from the summer of our being to the winter.

Grieving the Loss of Connection

When a significant threat or a loss happens, we suffer and grieve for the part of ourselves that has been threatened or lost. We may be angry or sad, tearful or exhausted. We may well focus on that which we lost – be it a person, the job or the place – however, it is the resulting fracturing of our identity that causes our suffering. Our suffering is directly comparable to the degree by which our identity has been threatened or fractured by threat or loss.

Clinical psychologist and researcher Professor Mike Powers explored the relationships between goals and depression throughout the 1990s. Powers found that the impact of losing a goal is directly related to the degree to which we define ourselves by that goal, more than any objective measure of the goal size. Simply put, Power's clinical psychology research supported the notion that we do not grieve for the person or thing we lose, rather we grieve for the loss of the relationship we had with that person or thing. This means that when a relationship contributes to our understanding of ourselves in the world, our identity is fractured when that relationship is damaged or lost.

Similarly, the work of Professor Glynis Breakwell has helped me to understand the relationship between identity and loss. Breakwell is a highly acclaimed social psychologist, an expert in identity, and, luckily for me, was the head of my psychology department when I was studying in Surrey in the late 1980s. She not only inspired me with her social psychology lectures, she gave me a summer job, and taught me with many quick-witted comments and insightful anecdotes.

In her pioneering 1986 book *Coping with Threatened Identities,* Breakwell argues that the majority of depressive episodes can be attributed to the experience of a threatened identity. She suggests that, when struggling with grief, we need to acknowledge the fracture that has happened *within* us, more than the loss that has happened *to* us. It is not enough to stop wanting the return of all we have lost: we need to regain a sense of ourselves in order to heal.

The Things People Say

When I was a child, my father was a huge believer in the power of quotes and sayings to teach us about the fundamentals of living a good life. Forever ingrained in me is the 'mock' Latin quote: 'noli illegitimi carborundum'.

This saying was popularised by US General "Vinegar Joe" Stilwell during World War II. He is reputed to have learned it from British army intelligence. Loosely translated, it means 'Don't let the bastards grind you down.' My father often used this phrase to suggest that I mentally rise above the criticisms of those I did not respect. It helped...sometimes.

In contrast, every time I looked longingly at something that my father might have considered a frivolous purchase, such as a pair of shiny new shoes, I would be met with 'a fool and his money are easily parted'. This long-established phrase is thought by some to have its origins in Proverbs 21:20 of the King James Version of the Bible. Others believe it has been around since the 16th century and was first used in 1573 by English poet Thomas Tusser. The word 'fool' was also the name of a popular English dessert from my childhood. Hence, at best, it conjured up images of blended custard and rhubarb, at worst it was a word that is decidedly cringeworthy. Still, my father, and his sayings, were born of another time.

Then there was 'laugh and the whole world laughs with you... cry and you cry alone' found in Ella Wheeler's 1883 poem 'Solitude'. This was a quote I despised. My father used it to encourage me to cheer up when I was obviously upset about something. It felt like salt in the wound.

Another quote he was fond of was 'rules are made for the guidance of wise men and the obeyance of fools'. Despite also referencing 'fools', this is a quote I really like. It echoes in my head when I am busy challenging the status quo and fighting against antiquated education policy.

One popular quote that never made it into my father's repertoire was 'what doesn't kill you, makes you stronger'. This well-known saying attributed to the German philosopher Friedrich Nietzsche attempts to reassure us of the positive possibilities arising from negative situations. It asks us to consider our failures as opportunities to learn and become more resilient.

I get the intention but I strongly challenge the sweeping use of this statement in everyday life. Yet, the quote is so popular, I fear it has led to the false belief that failure is, in fact, success in disguise. It is not.

I can see that it is important to embrace mistakes as a means to mastery. It is vital that we are prepared to experience the lows, so that we can climb to the highs. Progress is indeed rarely linear (to paraphrase another saying), and no success ever arrived without some healthy failing along the way. But I also think it incredibly naïve, and even dangerous, to reframe all trauma and struggle as somehow always nurturing strength and growth. There is an enormous difference between a setback and a calamity. And an enormous difference between 'moving on' when healing versus 'moving on' when still in pain.

Born in 1930, my father spent the first half of his adolescence amid World War II, and the second half of those most informative years dealing with the grief of so much life lost, as well as hardships such as food rationing and economic chaos. In his twenties, he battled the debilitating and life-threatening disease polio and became the only member of his ward to walk out of hospital alive. Years later, in his forties, despite being supremely fit, he caught a near-fatal heart virus which led to years of rehabilitation. The hospital doctors told him he had six months to live but, once again, my father defied potentially lethal infection. I am glad to say he went on to enjoy a rich meaningful life into his mid-eighties.

I look back on my father's life and consider that it was a life filled with required resilience. He certainly demonstrated a staggering degree of physical strength. His continual zest, insatiable curiosity and sense of adventure also highlighted a great deal of psychological stamina and flexibility. At its most simple and basic level, resilience is about hope, and my father was always interested in life, and generally hopeful.

Yet, it was not the tragedies and the traumas that created my father's ability to live with resilience, even though they certainly tested it to the limit. Rather, my father's resilience was built upon the successes of his life. Upon his ability to be interested in the adventure, no matter where it took him. He revelled in the connections he made, the relationships he built, the things that he learned and the wonder of the world around him.

His significant health issues held him back, zapped his energy and created an avalanche of other issues financially, socially and personally. My father developed depth from his experiences of trauma but found joy in the details of his life *in spite of* falling badly, not *because* of it.

The Pressure to Heal

There is no research that I can find that demonstrates that experiencing repeated tragedy will build psychological strength *unless* time and care is put into making a successful recovery. Significant trauma wounds people. It creates vulnerability and results in emotional scars that can last a lifetime. Children and adults who have survived trauma need a calm, caring and nurturing environment more than ever, not less than before.

Trying to minimalise the impact of falling badly can lead to far-reaching negative outcomes. A well-meaning 'hey, if it doesn't kill you...' can be so damaging if delivered before healing has occurred.

Traumatised people who are not given space and time to heal are more likely to become angry, unforgiving, unhappy and unwelcome in their world. They are more likely to feel alienated, misunderstood and alone. It is vital that we do not try to 'cheer' someone to recovery, without letting them take time to experience the pain of their situation, and then to heal. It is vital that we do not attempt to restore hope with misplaced beliefs in the power of the destructive to be creative. When bad things happen, the resulting fracture to our identity needs acknowledgement. Skills need to be relearned, perceptions slowly shifted, and then – gently, kindly, willingly – hope needs to be rekindled. People who live with unprocessed trauma live with unmet needs.

This undeniable truth does not mean that every impact of trauma is bad. Suffering significant trauma often leads to humility and a greater compassion for others. Recovery can bring a greater appreciation for life and a sense of gratitude for all that is well in the world. When given the time and guidance needed for healing, young people who have experienced trauma often grow up with a notable sense of purpose and passion. Never has this been more true than for world class tennis player Jelena Dokic, who, having been horribly abused as a child, found her way through her grief and pain to embrace enormous passion and purpose in life.

Significant trauma can incite a desire to change the world for the better, when healing has happened well.

So perhaps the quote should be, 'If it doesn't kill you, it can indeed make you stronger... if the trauma was minor and manageable, or healing has been careful and successful.' When handled with care, disruption can lead to reflection, which in turn can lead to a more creative way forward. But let us not forget that, when significant, trauma can be painfully destructive and damaging. Successful recovery from a bad fall takes time, considerable support, and gentle understanding.

If something matters, it matters when we lose it, no matter what it is.

Personally, I like to recount a more recent quote written by Havelock Ellis in his 1973 book 'Affirmations': 'The art of living lies in a fine mingling of letting go and holding on.'

I think my father would have approved.

SIXTEEN

Recovery, Reparation and Resilience

THERE IS A VAST body of information offering advice on how we might recover well from the impact of trauma and loss. For example, the work of Professor Aaron Beck exploring the impact of thoughts on our feelings, still forms the basis of much psychotherapy today. Aaron Beck is often considered to be the father of modern approaches to psychotherapy, namely Cognitive Behavioural Therapy, or CBT. His research and clinical practice during the 1960s was revolutionary, shifting ideas of therapy from deep psychoanalysis over one or more years; to six weeks of effective cognitive guidance. Simply put, Beck's CBT is based on the belief that our feelings are guided by our thoughts. If we are upset about an event, this is because of how we think about the event, rather than the event per se. For example, if you think not getting a job means 'I am unemployable and worthless' you will feel far more upset than if you think 'This is frustrating but I will find something that fits me better.' Or, if you think breaking up with your partner means 'I will never find another relationship. I will be alone forever', you are going to be far more upset than if you think: 'I am unsure what will happen in the future for me romantically. I may need to invest more heavily in my relationships with friends for a while'. Thus, if we can learn to rethink and reframe an unhelpful interpretation of an event in a more realistic and helpful way, we will feel better about it. Beck is not suggesting that we should reframe negative events as wholly positive. Rather, he believed that we will be less upset, and consequently more resilient, if we learn to catastrophize less and reduce the negative assumptions we make about the impact of an event that distresses us.

Thus, traditional cognitive behavioural techniques often involve challenging the catastrophizing thoughts we may have when we face adversity. Once we become aware of the all-consuming, distressing impact of unhealthy thoughts we can learn to challenge and change them for more realistic and helpful ones.

Other cognitive techniques help us to learn to focus on what we can control, rather than on what we cannot, when adversity strikes. The more we focus on aspects of life out of our control ('Will he love me again?' 'Why didn't I do or say something different?' etc) the more we feel out of control. In contrast, focusing on our attitude and how we can move forward well is within our control and can help us feel more agency in a difficult situation, and more hopeful.

The Body-Mind Connection

Those interested in the relationship between physical and mental well-being have focused more on the importance of caring for our physical selves to support our psychological selves. Certainly, the more we understand about the relationship between mind and body, the more we learn about the importance of lifestyle in supporting our emotional reactions and moods. For example, Professor Felice Jacka from the Food and Mood Centre, based at Deakin University in Australia, is one of a growing number of academics finding strong correlations between the food we eat, how we feel and our capacity to cope when things go wrong.

It makes sense to try to maintain a healthy diet of natural wholefoods, always get adequate sleep and do some exercise, especially when life is tough. Unfortunately, it is when we are the most stressed that we tend to crave the most wine, chocolate or ice cream, have the least motivation to exercise and have the most trouble getting to sleep. Thus, although we can certainly help ourselves have more emotional stamina and strength by being physically healthy, it is also important that we have self-compassion and are sympathetic to our primaeval reactions to threat. Over thousands of years we have evolved to crave high-calorie food, hide away and prepare for bad times when we are experiencing threat. This is so we are well prepared if we need to hide from an angry mammoth, fight a hungry sabre tooth tiger, or speedily run away from a starving bear. However you meet, numb or placate your wants and needs when you are highly stressed or distressed, remember to always go gently, and be kind to yourself.

The Power of Now

Others suggest we can find our most meaningful reparation and resilience in the details of life. They encourage us to learn to 'take a break' from focusing on the pain of struggle. In doing so, we need to remind ourselves to breathe in the moment, and to acknowledge the beauty of the 'little things'. For example, even when we are consumed with the pain of loss, a hot cup of coffee, the smell of rain or a shared moment of humour can give us a mental mini-break from the unbearable weight of distress.

As we progress, taking a few hours to do something fun can make an enormous difference to our capacity, without dishonouring a longer term need to grieve. Be it an episode of a favourite TV show, a drink with a friend, or a walk with the dog, small moments of nurturing distraction can provide us with a reminder of the value of life, and a valuable mental break. Certainly, evenings spent in the company of good friends have helped me through everything from a bad day at work to the awful experience of losing someone I love.

All roads to recovery – be they physically or psychologically focused – are meaningful when they support a process of reparation and reconnection, both within us, and between us and the world. They are meaningful because they help us to regain a sense of our whole-being, be it through our thoughts, our behaviour, our social connection or a more spiritual experience.

Acknowledge, Accept, Connect, Trust

I believe that embracing a process that best honours the constantly changing cycle of our identity creation, fracture and re-creation is vital to our long-term ability to be resilient, no matter what adversity or losses we face.

This process can be conceptualised in four steps. These are:

Step One: Acknowledge

No matter what paths we choose on our journey to recovery, we need to ensure we begin with awareness, acknowledgement and honouring of our fractured identity.

Step Two: Accept

In order to be able to let go of anything – from a broken relationship to a lost job – we need to be able to deeply understand that everything changes in life. In doing so, we learn to live with flexibility in an impermanent world.

Step Three: Connect

As we begin to heal, we need to begin to connect with our social world once more. This is not about re-creating the same connections that were threatened or lost: it is not about replacing a lost romance with a new one, or a lost job with another. Rather, it is about finding ways to connect with the social contexts of our lives so that we have our needs met and feel whole.

Step Four: Trust in Yourself

When things have gone wrong, it can seem artificial and unrealistic to contemplate 'everything being alright' in the future. Indeed, some adversity leads to long-term turmoil and devastation, especially when that adversity involves the loss of our health and the need to face our own mortality.

Moreover, even if things are going well, or our adversity seems manageable, it is foolhardy to trust that life will not be hard at some point in the future.

No matter what challenges life brings, if we can develop trust and faith in ourselves, and learn to listen to our inner voice, we can move forward well.

SEVENTEEN

Acknowledge – If it Matters it Matters

RECOVERY FROM ADVERSITY AND loss begins with the acknowledgement and honouring of the impact of that adversity and loss.

Acknowledging and accepting our personal reaction to trauma allows us to better understand how our identity has been threatened and altered by loss, and to subsequently heal ourselves well.

Prepare to Feel Deeply

This process is not about wallowing in self-pity or drowning in a sea of inaction forevermore. Nor is it about being unable to function or being too overwhelmed to find a way forward. Rather, it is an immediate uncovering and understanding of our fractured self, so that we can heal. It is not for the faint hearted. We need to be prepared to feel deeply when we sit with our wounds. This may mean hours of distraught weeping, sitting with seething anger, or spending time in quiet reflection. There are no rules, other than the rule to be true to our own experience of loss. If our loss is deep, then this process runs deep, and takes time.

Some of us might channel our emotions into being ridiculously busy. Others of us will feel frozen, unable to do much at all. We may feel the need to be alone more, or in contrast, to be with someone constantly close by. This is a time to put aside any perceived social pressure to be seen to be managing our grief in any particular way. There are no rules other than to ensure we do what is right for us, to prepare ourselves for reparation and recovery.

We know that the more we have learned to define ourselves by a connection, the deeper the distress we will experience when that connection is fractured or threatened. When the connection is with something in our context, it occurs within one or more of the four pillars of context I introduced in chapter 12: people, policy and practice, social norms or physical space. For example, the loss may be a relationship, a job, or moving out of a much-loved home.

The sense of loss, of fracture, we experience is not dependent on any objective measure of the worth of a connection. It is measured on how much that connection defined us, how much it met our key needs, and ultimately how much it supported our wellbeing. As such, it makes no sense to say to our grieving child 'it was just a rabbit' or to say to a grieving teenager, about the loss of a relationship, 'there are plenty more fish in the sea'.

Feeling Loss is Normal and Healthy

The deeper the threat or fracture to our identity, the more we feel distress, sadness and grief. For example, if we lose a relationship with someone we strongly identify with, we will be more deeply impacted than if we lose someone who we were less defined by, no matter how good or bad the relationship seemed. As such, grief and loss are extensions of the investment we place in others and in the broader world around us. When something matters it is because it has become a part of us, it has contributed to our socially constructed self, for better or worse. When we lose something that matters, reparation takes time.

Rather than embracing healthy humans as beings with a plethora of rich emotions, modern society has tended to label some emotional experiences as 'bad' and others as 'good'. As such, many of us feel bad or weak about feeling sad. Feeling appropriately unhappy during a disruptive or distressing interruption in connection is a healthy, strong and important response.

If we do *not* allow time to explore, accept and honour our emotional experiences, our wounds do *not* disappear on their own. They lie in hiding, causing us to feel acute moments of pain if the world moves even slightly the wrong way. Perhaps we find ourselves crying at the momentary loss of our car keys or shouting at the children because they forgot to tidy up. Our unaddressed wounds also stop us feeling whole and connected within ourselves, and with the world. When we constantly ignore a fractured identity, we become increasingly demotivated, disengaged and disconnected with life.

Allowing the Experience

It is so tempting to want to cheer ourselves, and indeed our children, 'out of distress'. Yet, if we start telling a distressed person that 'things are not that bad' or to 'cheer up because it is all going to be OK', we are in danger of minimising or dismissing the reality of their emotions. Even worse, if we tell a grieving person to 'toughen up' or 'be strong' we are ignoring the strength and the courage it takes to honour an authentic response to threat.

Far better to support someone who is suffering by allowing them to experience their emotional pain, their way. This means holding back from offerings of how 'everything is going to be fine'. People in distress need to know they are seen and heard without judgement or minimisation . They can then start to let go of their distress and move towards meaningful reparation.

An expression of sadness can be a beautiful way to express connection to something lost, an important means of self-care in the face of adversity, and a cathartic way to hold grief.

Once we take the time to acknowledge our emotional experience, we become better equipped to function well, no matter what life throws our way. We can ensure we don't end up feeling bad about feeling bad; or worse still, lost in avoidance or a pressing need to 'numb life'.

The more we honour our feelings of loss and grief in the face of adversity, the more effectively we can begin to repair, reconnect and regain a sense of our whole-being, one moment at a time.

Molly's Fish

My daughter Molly's first ever pets were four small shimmery fish. To Molly's delight, her fish were all 'mollies'. Sadly, after only six months of having fish in the family, tragedy struck. Molly's younger sister, Tess, accidentally 'fed' the mollies some glitter – which looked remarkably like the fish food, only with more sparkles. Neil and I found one of the fish dead, floating in the tank, while the girls were at school.

To minimise Molly's distress, we scooped the small lifeless being out of the tank and placed it in a sandwich bag in the fridge before she got home. This may seem an odd place to put a dead pet, but we wanted to tell Molly what had happened carefully and kindly. We also wanted her to have the choice of a fish funeral, or not. And quite frankly, we selected the fridge as a resting place because it was a warm day.

We certainly didn't want to minimise Molly's experience because we, as adults, were not upset about the fish dying. There were no thoughts of 'it is only a fish' or 'there are three others in the tank'.

This little being was our daughter's first pet. It had a name and had been given a place in our home. However, neither did we want to get out of giving bad news to our small daughter. We did not want to pretend the fish had swum away to 'some other lovely place' or had 'gone on holiday'. Rather we wanted Molly to have the opportunity to deal with a genuine loss and the reality of impermanence. Much like my parents had done with me, when he did not pretend that my beloved dog Simon had gone to some kind of canine Disneyland.

When Molly arrived home from school, we sat her down and told her that, very sadly, the fish had eaten some glitter and had died.

Understandably, Molly burst into tears and immediately declared that she had loved the fish. Still, once calm, she was amazingly understanding about the glitter mistake and seemed to regain her composure quickly. I suggested we could hold a fish burial and put the fish in the garden. Alternatively, I said I could quietly dispose of him.

Molly has always found it hard to make decisions under pressure, and this was no exception. After an hour of deliberating, she still didn't know what to do. So, to ensure we were not adding stress to distress, I suggested we keep the fish in the freezer for four weeks. I said that during this time she could decide what to do, and we would honour her need to say goodbye in whatever way worked best for her. I also said that if no decision had been made at the end of four weeks, I would make the final call.

Two weeks later, Molly was invited to sit in a circle in her classroom with the other students, to discuss family pets. Each child was asked to let everyone know if they had a pet, and if so what kind. They were then invited to say something about the pets they chose to mention. Many of the children talked animatedly about much loved family dogs or cats; some mentioned bunnies and Guinea pigs. Some of course, didn't have a pet (which must have made this topic a bit of a challenge). When it was Molly's turn she smiled broadly and declared to the class: 'I have a fish and we keep him in the freezer'.

When I went to collect Molly from school that day, the teacher stopped me with a puzzled look. She smiled and said: 'I hope you don't mind but I just have to ask....?'

If this were not surreal enough, over the following week two of Molly's school friends came over for a playdate. Not long after their arrival they excitedly asked if they could see Molly's fish from the freezer and give it a stroke… I obliged…I also realised that Molly was fine about the fish being dead. Another week passed, and I removed the fish from the freezer and disposed of it quietly.

The Rabbits

Four years later, on a sunny Christmas morning in 2016, we surprised Molly with a new pet, a small lop-eared grey rabbit. Molly, now nearly ten, had been campaigning heavily for a new pet for more than a year. At last her dream had come true.

Over the next few weeks, Pluto became a much-loved pet, hopping around our home, outside and in. During the day he would leap around the garden as if featuring in a Disney movie. Once evening arrived, he would often sit on the couch with us while we watched TV. He was thankfully completely house trained within days, and very much adored.

Six months later, Tess was given her own lop-eared pet on her seventh birthday. Fluffy Pluto fell in love with the small soft 'Moon'; and the two rabbits became inseparable.

The advanced cognitive capacity of the rabbits, compared with that of the fish, along with their fluff and cuddle-ability, resulted in both girls becoming very attached to them. Whenever Molly needed to work out a problem with friends, or felt emotionally overwhelmed by something, she would retreat to her room with Pluto. I remember her telling me that Pluto was the perfect listener. He never interrupted. Rather he always seemed to calmly understand how she felt and invited a definite opportunity for emotional co-regulation and connection.

Still, as with all things wonderful, they are always finite. Tragedy struck once more in 2017 when Pluto was just eighteen months old, and before Moon had even had a first birthday.

Both rabbits contracted myxomatosis.

This cruel and relentless, manufactured virus could be treated, but not legally in Australia. So, there was nothing we could do. For two weeks, I fed first Pluto and then Moon with a syringe, administered eye drops , antibiotics and love; but to no avail. Eventually Neil and I had to take the rabbits to the vet to be put down.

Both Molly and Tess were devastated. They cried, they moped, they hid away. I spent hours hugging Molly and talking about the pain of grief. I felt her pain. I felt both my daughters' pain. This time, unlike with the frozen fish, there was real grief in the air. Once again, it was so important not to minimise the girls' feelings. We made sure we did not say 'we can get another one' or 'it was only a rabbit'.

Just as my parents had done with a seven-year-old me after the loss of Simon, now it was my once again my turn to honour my children's feelings and make sure I did not hurry them to feel happier with a well-intentioned but misplaced 'time to move on' or 'come on, cheer up'.

It was around this time that I remember realising the deeper messages within Michael Rosen's 1989 children's book 'We're Going on a Bear Hunt'. The book tells the story of a family traversing many different terrains in their search for a bear. Each time they face a new type of environment, be it water, forest or mud, they must realise that they can't go over it, under it or around it. They have to go through it to reach their destination.

Certainly, when it came to losing their much-loved pets, both our younger two girls 'needed to go through it' to get over it.

Sometimes we lose something or someone and we genuinely move forward easily. When this happens, it is most likely that we were not overly connected to the thing or person we lost. Molly was not particularly connected to any of her fish, despite being excited at owning them. And that is of little surprise. Connecting to a fish is, after all, not an easy task.

I remember a close friend losing her father and never shedding a tear. This was not because of any denial or because of her being thick skinned or 'strong' but rather because she was not deeply connected to him. He had been absent for large chunks of her childhood, both physically and emotionally, and they had never had a deeply meaningful relationship. My friend was sad following her father's death and left wondering why he had not been more available, but her identity had remained largely intact.

In contrast, our daughters' reaction to losing their pet rabbits may seem over the top to some, even ridiculously dramatic when there is so much 'real trauma' happening in the world. But Molly strongly identified with her rabbit, as did Tess with hers. The girls needed to grieve to honour their threatened identities, the real loss they had experienced. And it was within those authentic experiences that they were able to find a way to feel whole again, and to grow wiser and stronger and more compassionate to others.

One day, hopefully well into the future, all three of my daughters will have to face other, more significant relationship losses – perhaps the loss of romances, best friends; and one day, they will almost certainly have to deal with the loss of Neil and me, their parents. When these times come, I hope they draw on their experiences as children dealing with the loss of loved pets, broken friendships and grandparents.

If they can do this, they will better understand that, big or small, grief is a process, and honouring your experience is the first step to moving through, and moving on, well.

I am certainly not suggesting that all dead fish should be stored in the freezer. Nor am I suggesting that every child will react the same way, with the same intensity to the loss of a pet rabbit. Some will barely notice the loss of a pet, a family friend or even a grandparent. Others will weep deeply for the loss of loved animals, broken friendships and extended family.

The deeper the connection, the deeper the grief, and that is neither good nor bad, right nor wrong.

Knowing how to honour our authentic experience to loss, without judgement, is a vital step towards reparation and recovery.

EIGHTEEN

Accept – Everything Changes

ONCE WE HAVE GIVEN ourselves time to honour the impact of adversity or loss, it is important we learn to accept that what has happened cannot be undone, and in fact, bad things happen to us all. Be it accepting a relationship is over, or that a failure cannot be undone, acceptance is a powerful part of being resilient. Moreover, once we can accept adversity and loss in our lives, we can begin to heal well, rather than move on internally broken, merely surviving our pain.

Despite its importance, acceptance can be undeniably tough to achieve. If you are struggling with a loss that seems wholly unwanted or unfair, then accepting that loss may seem totally unrealistic or even inappropriate. But, nonetheless, acceptance is an essential step to reparation and wellbeing. Once we can accept adversity and loss, even if we are deeply hurt by it, we can begin to slowly re-emerge into the world with the authenticity, willingness and courage required to reconnect. In doing so, we can begin to discover hope and move forward hopefully.

Acceptance is not about forgetting what we have lost, or what the loss meant to us. It does not diminish the importance of the relationship we had, or the thing we didn't manage to get, nor does it minimalise our suffering. Rather, acceptance means knowing that time cannot be reversed, that loss happens to us all, that everything changes.

Everything Changes

Buddhist monk Shunryu Suzuki Roshi is frequently described as one of the most influential teachers of Buddhism to have lived, largely because he is credited with bringing Zen Buddhism and philosophy to the western world. Shunryu was born in 1904 and grew up as the son of a traditional Zen Buddhist priest in rural Japan. In 1959, he moved to the US and, in the mid 1960s, founded a Zen Mountain Center in California. This mountain retreat was the first Buddhist monastery for Westerners and became home to many students over the next fifteen years. During this time, Shunryu transformed himself from a simple monk to a renowned leader.

David Chadwick, a Zen priest ordained by Shunryu in 1970, has since shared many of his teachings with a wider international audience. In his 2001 book 'To Shine One Corner of the World', he recounts many enlightening stories from Suzuki's teaching. The following one is particularly well known among Shunryu's followers:

> *"Suzuki Roshi, I've been listening to your lectures for years,"*
> *a student said during the question- and-answer time following*
> *a lecture, "but I just don't understand. Could you just please*
> *put it in a nut- shell? Can you reduce Buddhism to one phrase?"*
> *Everyone laughed. Suzuki laughed. "Everything changes," he*
> *said. Then he asked for another question."*

'Everything changes.'

This deceptively simple statement contains a lifetime of wisdom for living well, and for being resilient.

This Too Shall Pass

The day my first child was born, I had the instant realisation that having a baby was not all about me; it was all about this precious new being. This epiphany set the scene for my life with my new daughter from that moment forward.

Those first few weeks were a joyous time of swimming in a tide of contentment and flowers but also, like almost every new mum, trying to manage with very little sleep. Absolutely, I loved Lucia madly, but Lucia, at four months old, still didn't like to sleep for more than an hour or so at a time. And I wasn't a mother who was willing to let my baby cry. So I didn't.

I was there when Lucia woke. I was there when she fell back to sleep. Every day and night, for better or worse.

As time passed and my exhaustion increased, I would struggle to walk under the seemingly increased force of gravity that every lost hour of sleep created. My brain felt muddled and my mood wavered. But still I stood firm with my baby in my arms, just about all the time.

Lucia did not sleep through the night until she was nearly two years old. During those two long years not only did she sleep in short bursts, she never, ever wanted to be alone. And I never, ever wanted her to feel alone, not even for a minute. We consequently found ourselves in an all-encompassing codependency. Be it day or night.

The costs of this entwined, twilight lifestyle resulted in my feeling completely overwhelmed; but still the benefits of motherhood felt so incredibly great. It all still felt so ridiculously worthwhile.

I became more whole, even though the loss of my other roles in life left a hole inside of me. I had become a mother.

Towards the end of the first year of new motherhood, I remember asking a friend, a fellow new mother with a wakeful baby, how she coped with these relentless, exhausting times. She told me she had pinned a note to her fridge. Something to read as she grabbed for more chocolate to see her through...

The note said: 'This too shall pass'.

When Lucia finally started to sleep for longer stretches throughout the night, so did I. My energy returned quickly along with my capacity for all things. Neil and I consequently decided it would be great to have another baby, and to do it all over again.

Molly, my second daughter, was born when Lucia was three and a half. She was also a baby who woke frequently, but thankfully less often than her older sister had.

Another two-and-a-half years later Tess, my third daughter, came along. I remember being nervous about yet more potential sleep deprivation. Especially now I had a six year old about to start school and a strong-willed and curious toddler. Yet, I was also aware that I didn't want to be a different parent. I wasn't the person to shut the door, ever, for better or worse. In all honesty, I have become increasingly unsure if my way was the 'best way' to be a new parent; but for me, it was the only way, every time.

Luckily for me, at only two weeks old, Tess amazed us all and slept for six hours straight every night. At just two months, she was happy to sleep all night long.

They are who they are. They were who they were. 'And it all too did pass.'

Of course, at some level, we know that everything changes all the time. We know that time passes, that all life and experience is temporary. But to really realise and live with this *knowing*, rather than simply this knowledge, is a much rarer thing.

Some things change faster than we might like. Consider the last few days of a holiday slipping past with increasing speed or the last minutes of a special date disappearing like sand through our fingers. In contrast, other things don't change as quickly as we would like them to. We may desperately wish time away during a boring day at work or long for an end to a lengthy wait in a queue. Yet, despite our desire to either slow down or speed up the inevitable passing of time, it is still desperately hard for most of us to really 'know' that time will always pass, and everything will always change. It is hard for us to really 'know' that everything is impermanent and will ultimately be lost. Everything. Even us.

Why Me? – Holding on to Resentment

So many of us still feel cheated, surprised or angered when life changes suddenly or unpredictably, especially when the change involves the loss of something that matters. Certainly, when I have lost something or someone who really mattered to me, I have sometimes thought 'Why me?' 'Why now?' or 'What could I have done differently to prevent this from happening?' I haven't just felt a sense of loss, I have also experienced a sense of injustice, resentment or failure.

When a treasured boyfriend I had in my twenties ended our relationship, I remember feeling not simply sad, but angry and affronted that something I wanted so much could be gone. I spent inordinate amounts of time spinning imaginary scenarios around in my head about who had said what, and about what I could have said or done differently. I was looking for the problem that had caused the end, which had caused me to feel hurt; and which all seemed so unfair. Perhaps if I had been more accepting of the impermanence of all things, I would still have been sad for a while, but I would not have been so offended by the loss. I would not have been so desperate to hold on to what was no longer working.

When we do not accept impermanence, unwanted loss always seems to have arrived too soon, and to be downright unfair. Moreover, when we lose something of value, we are often compelled to hold onto the negative feelings associated with the loss long after the loss has happened. It is as if, at some semi-conscious level, we believe all that we lost is still retrievable, if only we can keep that fracture in our identity open and raw.

We hold onto the resentful feelings, the disbelief and the emotional pain the loss created in us. We hold onto a sense of injustice about something important being no more. Long after the initial distress of the situation, we might still wonder if we could have stopped things changing, if only we had been different, life had been different, or we had done things differently. Without a 'knowing' of impermanence, the more we are affronted by a change we do not want, and the more we tend to relive the experience of loss for the long term.

Not only did I constantly think about the injustice of my lost relationship in my twenties, I felt upset and angry about it for a very long time. In all honesty, I was angry about losing the relationship for far longer than the relationship had lasted. I wasn't simply sad at losing the company of someone I valued, I was angry that this aspect of life which had once worked so well, had changed into something untenable. I was caught in self-defeating anger and disbelief for a very long time.

Even when life provides a beautiful moment in the present, we can easily find ourselves missing it entirely as we remain caught in thoughts of past loss, held captive in the memories of 'what has gone wrong'. We examine our losses, question them, try to unravel them. Sometimes we try to imagine how things might have been different to make it all less painful, to make us feel more powerful, less hurt, or to have stopped change from happening altogether.

I can remember my inability to see the magnificence of the scenery and landscapes of tropical Queensland when I moved to Australia from England, because I was so busy being homesick. I remember having to leave social events which would have nurtured my current connections because I was too consumed by the loss of another relationship. Or possibly distracted by my anger and resentment.

I have missed so many valuable and beautiful moments time and time again, instead caught desperately wanting some other world or to have had different expectations.

I have been caught in the imaginings of a life where loss doesn't happen. Yet, ironically, at the same time, I have found myself longing for the excitement of change. As if all unwanted change is unfair, yet all longed-for change is required to find purpose.

The relentless rumination that prevents us embracing the life we have now, passes when we learn to love what we have, while also accepting that one day it will be gone.

It took me a long time to be able to appreciate the value in relationships that had ended before I wanted them to. To accept that something could be great and yet also temporary. When I was younger, I unsuccessfully tried to make myself feel better about loss by minimalising everything that I felt upset about losing. My poor attempts to diminish the importance of my losses gave me a brief sense of my own power: a feeling of 'I'm just fine without it'. They didn't make the distress of loss go away. Rather, they resulted in my burying my emotions, holding onto debilitating resentment and cultivating a desire to 'live well in revenge' rather than simply to live well.

Recovery from a love lost is *not* about changing love or attachment into hate or disinterest; for example, saying 'I didn't love him anyway' or 'I never really wanted the job'. It is *not* about learning 'detachment'. Rather, reparation and resilience are about learning the power of 'non-attachment': how to love deeply and wholeheartedly while knowing things will change. Everything ultimately will be gone. As such, our ability to deal with unwanted loss is more about accepting impermanence and change, than it is about the diminishing of, or the denial of that which we had.

If we can truly accept the temporary, impermanent nature of all things, we may still feel sad when we lose them, but we are less likely to be caught with a sense of injustice, resentment or blame. We are less likely to constantly wish things had worked out differently, to constantly wonder if we could have somehow prevented change from happening, to feel a failure.

Acceptance Leads to Confidence and Connection

Moreover, when I think back to the romantic losses of my youth, I can see that I frequently accelerated the end of a relationship because I was so anxious about losing it. And therein lies the rub. There is an added irony of the constancy that arises when we are more accepting of impermanence and change. When we are less anxious about losing that which we are connected to, it tends to last longer. When we do not fear change and loss, we are more confident and attentive of what we have now. Our greater confidence and capacity to connect, means we are less likely to be rejected, disappointed or left agonising over our choices and behaviours.

It always strikes me that I didn't manage to establish a long term, loving relationship until I had reached a state of feeling fine about not having a relationship at all. I clearly remember the day before I first started dating Neil, when I declared to my cousin Pam that I had all my needs met, just as I was. I remember finally being at peace with being single. I can now see that my feeling comfortable to be single was what, in fact, enabled me to be less fearful about losing another romantic relationship. As I write this, my life and Neil's have been entwined, for better and worse, for 23 years. During the good times, I feel more deeply connected to Neil but also more confident in our status as two different beings. When times are hard between us, it is often when one of us is feeling more insecure about life, and the possibility of any change seems more foreboding and harder to bear.

It is easier to be resilient, and to live life to the fullest, when we know, *really know* – and really accept – that life is transient and everything changes, and that is OK. Imagine yourself watching a beautiful scenic view. What captures your attention when you look around you? Is it the consistency before you, the immovable land or the still trees? Or is it, perhaps, actually the things that change that capture your attention and interest the most? Possibly the gradual shifting of light and colours caused by a setting sun, or more dynamic changes such as a car coming and going, or a person walking by?

When we accept the impermanence of life, we are better able to embrace all that we love and to let go of all that we lose.

NINETEEN

The Art of Letting Go

IN 1999, AFTER SIX months of hard work and culture shock living in my new home of Queensland, I was beyond happy to welcome my parents for a visit as part of their extended trip to Australia and SE Asia.

We spent three fabulous weeks exploring my adopted country as tourists. This gave me the opportunity to see the beauty of the tropical waters; to embrace the adventure of the Tablelands and the excitement of fossicking for emeralds; to be in awe of the first night sky I had ever seen with the full glory of the milky way arching around us; and to laugh at all the things that simply didn't make sense to us English folk.

On the final day of my parents' visit, I felt sad that they were leaving me to fight alone in this strange land. I was also enormously sad to know it would be a long time before I saw them again. We ate a final dinner in celebration of the holiday, which finished with a large cheesecake. As thoughts of saying goodbye took hold, my mother and I ate pretty much the entire dessert between us; sharing our anxiety about living on different sides of the world, spoonful by spoonful.

As we ate, I couldn't help but notice how happy my Dad appeared. A stark contrast to my mother and me.

Curious, and slightly perturbed, I asked him how he felt about leaving.

'Very excited!' he replied, 'We are going to a beautiful Thai island that I have never been to before... can't wait!'

At the time I remember thinking my Dad seemed a lot less sad about leaving, than I felt about him going. I now know that he had absolutely loved our tropical adventure together; however, he understood and embraced the impermanence of life. Rather than always trying to hold onto a moment for just that little bit longer, he saw endings as opportunities to embrace new beginnings.

Change Happens

But how can we really know this, like my father did? How can we shift from a conceptual, intellectual understanding of change, to a more accepting and spiritual one?

Perhaps the only way to let go of a longing for constancy, is to find the eternity in each passing moment. We need to find the power of now, to accept the impermanence of life.

The more we can see what is real for us, here and now, the more we can understand change, even within the smallest moment. The more we experience and understand change, the more we feel whole and at peace with the ebb and flow of life. When we invest in 'now', we see the beauty in the details of each moment, because we notice those details, how they constantly change, and moreover, how it is the small changes that capture our attention and interest.

It always amazes me how differently I see Western Australia, my home after Queensland, when I have visitors. When I eagerly take family or friends out to show them the beauty of Perth, my home city, I am reminded to pay attention to all that is around me. I see the views all over again, the expansive blue skies and white beaches; the parrots and the palms. I take a moment to see the natural world and its universal beauty, and it always makes me feel better, not to mention immensely proud, of where I call home.

The more time we take to see ourselves and our world, the more we become aware of the richness of the everchanging, eternal 'now'. This means we spend less time debating the injustice of past losses, or, daydreaming about what new, improved stability we might create in the future. We become less desperate to be in control of life and to make it permanent.

Certainly there are times when I have an immense amount of stress going on in my life, but still, if I take the time to see my life in the moment, there is always beauty to be found in the transient details around me. Be it in the taste of a morning coffee, or my dog being forever and unconditionally happy to see me. To find pleasure in such small moments is not in any way to minimise how hard life can be as a whole; rather it is to understand the power of now.

The more we learn to stay connected to the moment, the more we learn to feel whole, no matter what change and disruption occurs in our larger, extended life.

There are several key ways we can find 'now' in our life, become more aware, more present, and therefore more knowing of impermanence.

The Power of Mindful Meditation

Mindful meditation is not only a key to self-awareness and self-knowing. As I discuss in Chapter Four; it is a powerful key to becoming more present in day-to-day life. A path to the freedom of living fully in the eternal 'now' of each moment.

Daisetsu Teitaro Suzuki, commonly known as DT Suzuki, was a Harvard professor and expert on Zen Buddhism. Although sharing a similar expertise, he is not to be confused with Shunryu Suzuki who I quoted in Chapter Seventeen. In DT Suzuki's 'Introduction to Zen Buddhism', he suggests that the idea of Zen is 'to catch life as it flows'. Similarly, we could say that the art of wellbeing is to do the same.

As such, meditation is arguably the most important practice we have for supporting our wellbeing and our resilience. Be it ten minutes of guided practice listening to a meditation app on your phone each night or ten minutes sitting counting your breath each morning. Be it western mindfulness practice or Zen meditation. Be it deliberate practice to increase love and compassion or simply a matter of taking a few moments to sit with your breath when you first wake in the morning.

Mindful meditation practice has become one of the most studied and supported pathways to wellbeing, and for good reason. Still, the power of meditation can seem bewildering and bring out skepticism in the best of us. When life feels overwhelmingly busy, the simple art of meditation can easily seem too simple to possibly be useful. We wonder if meditation is an outdated myth, and ask: 'How can learning to sit still be helpful in the complexity of "real" life?'

As we discussed in Chapter Four, mindful meditation is both deceptively hard and wholly simple, but it is also an incredibly powerful tool when practised regularly. Regular practice increases our self-awareness and our ability to connect with our internal and external world as both observer and participant. Yet, despite the wellbeing outcomes of meditation practice being great in themselves, mindful meditation is more a tool than it is 'the answer' in itself. The true power of meditation lies in its ability to help us understand both ourselves and our impermanence. It helps us to really 'know' that 'everything changes'. If you embrace and accept impermanence, you live more freely than if you do not. Mindful meditation is arguably the most powerful tool for learning the art of resilience that we have; however, it is not the only one.

Nature and Play

Some people can embrace change and impermanence without ever having participated in a mindfulness session. This may be because they have spent a lot of unstructured time learning to engage in life, possibly through play, or through time spent in nature growing up. Certainly, the importance of play and free time for us all cannot be understated. Time spent freely in nature encourages us to develop a sense of wonder and awe and to stay curious, whatever our age.

If ever there was a concern about how westerners spend their time in the twenty first century, it needs to include consideration of the importance of nature, creativity and play. It is vital that we ensure we all engage in free time, preferably outdoors without too many rules, structure or guidance from others. This is true for us no matter what stage of life we are in. It is, however, incredibly important in childhood, and hence very important to embrace in schools. True education begins with the opportunity to develop self-direction, curiosity, symbolism and passion for structured traditional teaching. As such, in my professional life I spend a lot of time suggesting schools step back from structured outcome-driven teaching and take free time, play and creativity more seriously.

I firmly believe that free time is not just 'time out from education' – it is a vital path to learning, adult happiness and life success. Wellbeing and self-determination begin within a context that values play in and of itself. Increasing numbers of studies are identifying significant links between the amount of free time a society allows its children, and the mental health of its young people. For example, Professor Peter Gray, an educational psychologist and an expert in childhood development, has written many influential works about the importance of nature for development and the importance of play, especially in natural settings. Gray, who is based in Boston, advocates for a greater emphasis on self-directed learning in children, with an emphasis on the many social, psychological and academic benefits of creative play.

Consider a time in your own life when someone made you laugh uncontrollably, or you ended up being gregarious and playful because you were caught up in the moment. How good did it feel when it happened? And more importantly, how pleasantly calm, connected and centred did you feel following your moment of play?

Flow and Engagement

Other people find their 'now' in engaging activities that allow them to experience a sense of flow, a concept defined and explored in depth by psychologist Professor Mihaly Csikszentmihalyi in his 1990 book *Flow: The Psychology of Optimal Experience*. The book describes the experience of engaging in an activity that dynamically fits well with our skills and ability. We can increase the difficulty of the challenge as our abilities develop. When we are in flow with an activity, time can seem to come to a standstill. We are in the moment, not caught up in other thoughts or distractions. We are embraced in our 'now'.

For me, flow comes when I paint. Painting calms and energises me in equal measures, it settles me, meets my needs for autonomy and competency, and helps me feel whole-heartedly immersed in the moment. When I finish a session at my painting class, the colours around me are more vivid. I see more of the beauty in the details of my world. I feel more alive.

Flow for you may be doing something entirely different. For example, it may be about playing rock music, swimming laps of the pool, writing thrillers or enjoying gardening. The power of flow as a tool to help us find our 'now' highlights the incredible importance of making time, every week, to do something we love.

The Struggle With Change

So many of us face a lifelong challenge to deal with change. We worry about everything from the loss of our keys to the loss of our youth and, ultimately, the inevitable loss of our lives. We see change as hard and unfair, and our inability to accept it leaves us struggling to be resilient when loss occurs.

If you are someone who, like me, has struggled to accept the inevitability of change and loss, then mindfulness meditation practice will help; but so too can nature, embracing unstructured time wholeheart-edly or simply, regularly doing something you love.

Investing in ways to discover the power of our ever changing 'now', helps us to find our eternity in the impermanence of life.

TWENTY

Flexibility

THE MORE WE UNDERSTAND impermanence, the better able we are to accept the ebb and flow of life with flexibility and authenticity. We become less overwhelmed when we face changes and challenges. We are better equipped to change our life course when required; meaning we are prepared to not only change plans but also to change our behaviour and to change our attitude as fits each new situation.

Moreover, the more we can understand the relationship between flexibility and impermanence, the more we will understand that being a steady and stable person is different from being an immovable or unchanging one.

When I was about fourteen, I joined a group of six or seven girls from my school for a weekend slumber party at the home of my then-closest friend. I still clearly hold onto the memory of that weekend, but for all the wrong reasons.

Shortly after the first evening began, I remember feeling horribly anxious. I was struggling to connect with the other girls largely because I was fearful of missing out the exciting sounding activities they were planning. Living in Themelthorpe, such a long drive from the nearest city, meant that I missed many social events. Nevertheless, despite knowing geography was the reason I couldn't join in, I still felt isolated, excluded and somehow 'not good enough' for my friends' world.

My feelings of overwhelm increased as the evening continued, and I became increasingly withdrawn. Eventually, unable to keep smiling, I ran from the discussions about shopping trips, parties and music.

I went into the bathroom, locked the door and wept.

For a few moments, I felt relief. I could finally stop pretending all was well. However, I was very aware that there is an acceptable amount of time to visit the bathroom without raising suspicion. I guessed I would have about five minutes before curiosity came running. Five minutes that were passing very quickly. The more I cried, the more I felt overwhelmingly separate from the other girls and their shared experiences. At one point, I remember taking a breath, looking in the mirror, and being brought back to tears by the sheer sadness of my own reflection.

As the minutes passed, it became increasingly evident to me that it had possibly been a bad move to walk off alone. I had gone into the bathroom without saying a word to my friends and had now been absent for a good ten minutes. The longer I continued to sit on the perfectly tiled, but incredibly uncomfortable bathroom floor, the worse my sense of isolation and hopelessness became; but also, the more awkward and frustrated I felt. I now desperately wanted to leave the bathroom, return to the group, and try to join in. But I didn't know how.

If I returned with a tear streaked, snotty red face, everyone would ask what was wrong. If I said 'nothing', then I would seem crazy to have been so upset; but if I said 'everything' then I would seem crazy for having 'issues'. In my school world, having poor mental health meant having something 'wrong with you'. Asking someone if they were OK, seemed more a judgement than a question.

Eventually, possibly twenty minutes later, someone knocked on the door and asked the dreaded 'no win' question: 'Helen? Are you alright?' I didn't know how to answer so I said nothing. I had obviously been in the bathroom for an unusually long time.

The well-meaning girl on the other side of the door asked me to come out. I suddenly felt frozen to the spot. I still said nothing.

My attempt to hide away was now causing me to become the centre of attention, in a very uncomfortable way. I could hear more voices. God. No. There was now a gathering outside the door. I decided to hide in the corner of the room I was already hiding in.

More time passed. Voices became more urgent. Teen girls are drawn to drama and I was being increasingly dramatic.

A whole hour later, the girls outside the door decided to elect two people to stay by the bathroom door, in the hope that I would come out knowing there was now only a minimal welcome committee. I was beside myself with anxiety... my previous overwhelm became relatively insignificant. I eventually shouted out that I needed to go home. I said I had vomited...it must have been something I ate...

My mother took a whole 45 minutes to come. I spent that entire time in the bathroom. When she eventually arrived, I silently unlocked the door and walked out. I kept my gaze down to avoid the intense eye contact of the girls, and the concerned if puzzled faces of my best friend's parents.

No-one believed I was physically unwell. I was obviously very emotional, and very embarrassed. The story of my 'crazy' behaviour circulated quickly and I became known as the girl who had a meltdown... and wouldn't come out of the bathroom...

To this day, part of me wishes I had immediately declared feeling physically unwell, as an instant, 'legitimate' means of escape. However, this would still have resulted in my separating myself from the people I was already feeling separated from; and increasingly trying to be someone I was not. If I had been more mature, self-accepting and confident, I could have simply told my friends I was struggling with living in a rural community, which was true. If I could have been more vulnerable, I could have been so much stronger. If I could have been more authentic, I would have authentically felt better.

But, expressing vulnerability to a group of teen girls can be a scary prospect at the best of times. Even more pressingly, I so, so wish that I had been able to be flexible in my thinking, behaviour and in my emotional reaction. I wish I had come out of the bathroom when that first girl had knocked. I could have said I was feeling sad, that I needed a moment. I could have said I was upset about school, about home, about anything.

How I wish I had managed to make a mental U-turn and said something, or really anything.

After all, there was no problem with having a problem. The problem is in not knowing how to express ourselves, address the problem, or manage our emotions so we can move on. In my teenage moment, I could have been a 'bit upset' and then got a 'bit better'... and the evening would probably have gone on uneventfully. The real drama of the situation was in the escalation of my distress and my inability to come out of the bathroom. I didn't know that being appropriately authentic makes you less of a target, not more of one. I didn't know that being vulnerable is not just possible, it is essential. I didn't know that everyone has worries, not just me. I didn't know that expressing myself honestly may have led to increased connections, workable solutions and my feeling better.

I didn't know how to stand up from an emotional fall. I didn't know how to be flexible and to change my mind.

I have told this story several times to each of my three daughters as they have entered the social complexities of pre-teen and teen life. Whenever one of my children is struggling to move on from emotional overwhelm, a poor choice, a tiny error or a gigantic mistake; I tell them it does not matter how emotional they have become. It does not matter how much they messed up, how much they wished they had made a different choice...

The important thing is knowing how to come out of the bathroom.

Psychologically flexible people not only support their own flexibility, they also allow others to be flexible. They are less likely to hold others to their opinions and plans in a fixed and judgemental way. Rather, they are more likely to allow others the flexibility to change their minds and their behaviours.

They are less likely to be frustrated, angry or resentful when things don't go to plan, or plans change. Rather they are more likely to feel calm and relaxed in a storm of change; and others are more likely to feel calm and relaxed around them.

Most importantly of all, flexible people are more able to flow within the changing weathers of our constantly changing lives. They are willing to change course when their thoughts, opinions or behaviours are leading in an unwanted direction. They are more likely to know 'how to come out of the bathroom'.

We can develop our psychological and emotional flexibility with practice, along with our cognitive flexibility. The more we learn new topics and skills, the more open to change and complexity we become. The more we do things that move us out of our comfort zone, while also feeling safe, the more we can learn to tolerate distress and deal effectively with unexpected events and novelty.

Similarly, meeting new people, travelling to new places or simply trying a new recipe for dinner all help us to stay open to change, and to stay connected within our world, no matter what the emotional forecast brings. When did you last have to be flexible and embrace a complete 'change of plan' in some area of your life? It can be hard to shift your focus when you didn't plan to, or really want to. Yet, the more we practise change, the more we build our flexible selves.

At some level, all learning requires challenge and change. As such, engaged learners of all ages are constantly learning to deal with the inevitability of change as they grow. They are learning to deal with the discomfort of not knowing something or being challenged by something new. They are also learning the value of new thoughts and ideas. Lifelong learning becomes a key to knowledge, skills and to lifelong psychological flexibility.

A Final Word of Warning

Despite the reality of flexibility being built on learning new things and facing challenge, it is important to be aware that not all challenges lead to positive development or are positively associated with learning the art of resilience.

Let's go back to one of my dad's favourite quotes: 'If it doesn't kill you, it makes you stronger'. Just as it is important to acknowledge that unexpected trauma does not necessarily build any capacity for resilience – especially if we do not give someone time to honour the extent of their pain and grief – it is also important to understand how careful we need to be when encouraging others to do difficult things which include novelty or change.

Pushing yourself out of your comfort zone can indeed encourage tolerance with discomfort, learning with flexibility and an acceptance of impermanence in all things. However, we need to experience some sense of *success* with our ability to master change and challenge, if it is to be helpful in our mastering the art of resilience.

Consider a child who does not want to run in the sports carnival at school. If that child is nervous because they are facing a manageable challenge, then it might well be helpful to encourage them to face their nerves and run. If they then make it across the finish line, even if in last place, their accomplishment may well help them to take future risks more easily, and develop a flexible attitude to life. Their experience will help them to learn the art of resilience.

If, however, a child is highly anxious about participating in a race, perhaps because they feel ashamed or embarrassed about running in public, this is a very different situation. If this child is coerced into running and they believe they are being laughed at or publicly embarrassed for their efforts, they are learning that challenge and change have distressing consequences. This child will seek survival by becoming less flexible and consequently less able to be resilient.

Thus, we need to be compassionate and flexible, when it comes to encouraging others to do things that make them nervous, be it our child running in the sports carnival or our colleague presenting at a conference. We need to be aware that people's perceptions of risk, safety and their corresponding levels of anxiety vary enormously, as do their contexts and their expectations.

Whereas one nervous child may benefit from doing their best in a foreboding debate; a highly anxious child left feeling embarrassed by a debilitating mental freeze, will not. Taking part in any stressful activity is only beneficial to learning the art of resilience if it reduces fear, rather than compounds it; and if it supports a sense of competency, rather than diminishes it. It is a great thing to encourage and cheer others beyond their comfort zone, but it is never a great idea to coerce or force others with a misplaced belief that having a difficult experience will somehow 'toughen them up'.

When we find the middle ground between comfort and fear, we find the place where we will grow flexible and strong.

TWENTY-ONE

Reconnect and Rebuild

"Perhaps the secret of living well is not in having all the answers but in pursuing unanswerable questions in good company."
– Rachel Naomi Remen

WHEN WE HAVE HONOURED and accepted a difficult experience with courage, care and flexibility, we then need to focus on healing ourselves as a social being; and this means creating healthy connections *externally*, so we can feel connected *internally*.

Healthy connections come in many guises, but they all have one key thing in common. They all meet one or more of our three key needs (as extensively demonstrated in research supporting Richard Ryan and Edward Deci's Self-Determination Theory):

1. Our need to experience authentic relationships with others as we develop belonging.
2. Our need to experience autonomy with a sense of ownership and control over our lives.
3. Our need to experience a sense of competency with the belief that we are growing and progressing in some way.

It is vital that we understand that healthy connections are not about the things we are connected to per se; rather their 'healthiness' is measured on the basis of how well they meet our needs. Once we understand this, we are better equipped to focus on how a connection, or a reconnection, makes us feel and think about life rather than what it 'looks' like, or who or what it is with. For example, when I moved to Perth I had experienced a number of very short lived highly unsuccessful relationships and was feeling very 'single'. I thought I really wanted a romantic relationship to make my life better, and felt inadequate that I didn't have one. I was also then in my early thirties, and my biological clock had started ticking loudly. Would I be single forever? Would I ever be in a relationship that lasted long enough to produce children? What was 'wrong' with me?

As a means of finding friends and the beginnings of a social life I joined a local drama group. I had always been interested in drama and the idea of acting; and thought it would be interactive enough to ensure I got to know other people in my new world.

The group turned out to be everything I hoped for and more. It was creative, stimulating and a whole lot of fun. I learned performance skills quickly, had an extraordinary opportunity to express myself through drama, and I made some great friends.

I remember waking up one Sunday morning and preparing to go to a rehearsal of the play in which I had recently been cast. In a sudden moment of clarity, I realised that I felt happy and content. I was no longer yearning for that elusive romance. Rather, all the things I wanted from this apparently unattainable, imagined relationship were the things I had found in my drama group. I had belonging, engagement and relevance. My needs were being met.

Of course, this meeting of my needs with my drama group ensured I felt very whole and well internally. This meant I must have become more approachable and easier to connect with. It seemed I had barely uttered the phrase 'I'm actually totally fine with being single' to my cousin Pam, when I met Neil. Neil and I quickly became a couple and then, two years later, parents.

When our external connections meet our three key needs for relatedness, autonomy and competency, we become internally whole; and that means we experience wellbeing.

Creating and recreating a strong web of social connections, be they many or few, ensures we can repair well from struggle and trauma. They also ensure we can hold onto a sense of who we are more fully when the going gets tough. As such, healthy connections define our life in the good times and prepare us for resilient living when adversity strikes.

This also reminds us that resilience is not about building some sort of impenetrable psychological armour that can protect us from loss. It is not about being 'tough or thick skinned' or relentlessly 'pushing on through'. Rather, it is about successfully letting the world *in* far more than it is about keeping it out. Being resilient involves having the courage to meaningfully connect, rather than the fear of avoiding connection. It is about flexibility, openness, vulnerability and the ability to deal with the knowledge that with gain, comes the potential for loss.

Our recovery from adversity is not simply about how we change and develop as an individual; it is not an isolated or solitary pursuit. It is just as much about the connections we form with others, the tasks we pursue and our wider sense of the world.

Resilient living has far less to do with any aspect of our individual functioning than we might like to think, and far more to do with how we fill the spaces between us.

TWENTY-TWO

Building Connection by Walking Away

CONNECTION IS THE KEY to living life well in all weathers, but only if it is authentic and within a healthy context that meets our key needs. Being disconnected from our context is a lonely place to be, but being connected to an unhealthy context can result in our feeling like we are the wrong person.

Certainly resilience sometimes requires us to learn how to connect more authentically and meaningfully within our context. We may need to work to connect with others around us in a more compassionate way, to understand and embrace the norms of our socially constructed environment, to comply with the rules and practices around us or to find greater beauty and familiarity within the physical space in which we reside.

Sometimes, however, the solution lies in finding a new, healthier context. Sometimes we work to create a strong web of social connections, but we remain fractured and unstable. We may experience an illusion of belonging, only to find that the web we have carefully constructed has been built in a place of constant shade, without the conditions to nurture us. We find that, no matter how hard we try, we feel alone and dissatisfied.

We may come to realise that we have built our web in a fragile or hostile environment – that our friends or partners really aren't very supportive, or are even undermining or toxic – and we find ourselves rebuilding, repairing and rethinking our connections to the point of exhaustion.

When, no matter how hard we try, we struggle to feel whole within the social web of our context, we may need to walk away so that we can connect to a different context—a different community or friend group – which better supports us, and forms a better fit with our inner voice. Just as I did when I walked away from my unhealthy marriage in my twenties.

This is not about giving up on the hard stuff or avoiding risk. This is about honouring our needs.

Sometimes, we need to seize the moment...and go someplace else.

TWENTY-THREE

Holding Hope – In Search of Possibility

THROUGHOUT THIS BOOK WE have explored the need to learn about the ever-changing seasons of our lives. To understand and embrace our own constant cycle of social identity creation, fracture and repair. We have learned that we need to develop ourselves with authenticity and integrity as a person in order to live well when times are good. We need to honour and accept our experience of fracture when adversity strikes. Finally, we need to learn how to reconnect and regain an experience of being a whole being once more.

At the heart of this cycle of 'being and becoming' lies hope. But what is hope? Surely it is naïve and possibly even dangerous to think everything is always going to turn out perfectly, right?

In Search of a Better Ending

During 2020, after the world was thrown unexpectedly and headlong into the pandemic, many schools in Australia employed the help of outside consultants, such as me, to support student and staff wellbeing.

Around August, I heard about a talk a colleague had presented to the staff and students of a local school. The takeaway message had been to 'keep hope alive'. The audience had been told that, no matter what, they needed to stay hopeful that all would be well in the end. They were told that holding hope would be the best way to support worried children and to keep family morale high.

I was very unconvinced.

Many things turn out to be more OK than we think they will be – or we survive them more intact than we believe we might have done – but this is not always the case.

Sometimes outcomes involve stress, distress and grief, which require acknowledgement and acceptance. And whether good or bad, they are often out of our control. We cannot make things around us turn out well simply by willing it to be the case.

Pam

My cousin stayed hopeful of a cure for her brain cancer right up to the time she lost her life from it. The hope she maintained reflected the optimistic and sunny disposition she had demonstrated her entire life; but still, it did not play out into a reality.

In the last six months of her life it became obvious that western medicine could do no more to help her, and so, remaining determined, she turned her attention to complementary and more alternative therapies. It was understandable, and I am sure she was not the first or last severely ill person to seek out options that they might not previously have considered worthwhile.

Her sister and parents identified a potential treatment sold in jars, to be consumed daily. They looked high and low for research to support the claims of this very pricey product, but evidence was scant at best.

My cousin asked me if, as an academic psychologist, I might be able to help find some published research. I was keen to do anything that might prove helpful, but I found myself faced with a horrible dilemma – what did helpful mean in this situation?

Ultimately, I reported back that there had been some trials that suggested the substance would do no harm, and may have potential as a cancer treatment, which was true. I also gently let her know that I could not find any published, peer reviewed research confirming its effectiveness.

At best, the jury was still out.

I told my cousin that even if this substance was effective when in contact with cancer cells, it had the problem of needing to reach her brain. Our bodies are well designed to keep our brains safe which means that the substance would need to be able to get across the brain's very protective blood-brain barrier.

Still, with few other options, my beautiful cousin proceeded to buy and ingest the substance daily.

A month or so after starting her new regime she said she felt better. She found it easier to walk, when she had previously been becoming very immobile. She had more energy and she felt more 'hopeful'.

In addition, her close family felt they were doing 'something' and that this something was relatively safe. It was not going to make anything worse, except their bank balance, and it might even make things better.

A few months later, in 2021, my cousin died. It appeared that any perceived improvements to her physical health had been short lived at best.

She was in her late fifties when her life ended. She left behind three children, including one still in her teens, two grandchildren, her partner, her sister, her parents and many other family members and friends. All loved her dearly and all were devastated, me included.

Things do not always turn out for the better and sometimes a silver lining is extremely hard to find. Sometimes we have no control over the fractures that happen to us.

Later in the same year, a friend of Neil's and mine discovered that her mother had developed the same type of cancer as my cousin had;

an inoperable brain tumour. Our friend was understandably distraught and desperate to support her mum. She asked if the substance my cousin had taken had 'worked' at all.

It was a hard question to answer.

My cousin's family had been left cynical about the expensive course of action, but on balance, they would probably do the same thing again, in the same situation. No matter how dubious these jars of hope had been as a possible treatment, they had made everything just that little bit easier to bear.

I told my friend that obviously my cousin had not survived her cancer, or even been granted much more time. She had however, been given a new lease of life when she started taking the substance daily. A lease of life fuelled by a belief that if you have a reason to hope, you have a reason to live.

I wondered if unrealistic hope is sometimes more important than realistic expectations.

My friend decided to seek out the treatment for her mother. She reported back that the cost of each small jar had now doubled.

It seemed the price of hope had risen with demand.

I was left wondering what it means to have hope, and indeed, how important hope is to our physical health and to our psychological well-being. Moreover, I wondered what having hope actually means?

Can it possibly support resilience to believe in something working out well when all hard evidence suggests it is not going to? As much as a positive spin might give someone a temporary sense of relief and positivity; what long term damage comes with denying the reality of loss? Maybe none, if your life is ending. Maybe a lot when it is not.

To blindly believe in a 'happy ever after' in every situation certainly makes no sense to me. Nor does pinning our 'hopes' on events outside of our control. As with the pursuit of happiness I discussed at the very start of this book, I believe the goal of always being cheerful, carefree and fortunate seems destined to lead to much disappointment. Yet, the jars of hope that my cousin bought made such a difference to her final months of being gravely unwell. They supported her need to believe in the possibility of recovery right to the very end.

Will it All be OK?

I intensely dislike being told that 'all will be fine', when all other evidence suggests it will not (or we have no way of knowing). Yet, I have found myself telling my children that all will be fine in the end, when they have fallen out with a friend, or done badly in an important school test. It is so tempting to say to suffering people 'it is all going to be OK', as if we have the power to bring a positive end to a situation and make those suffering feel instantly better.

So why do we insist on telling others that their life will be fine? And what do we really 'hope' to achieve by saying this? Are we simply enacting a misplaced and uncomfortable desire to avoid a distressing conversation?

Do we think that a confident nod to future wellbeing will help people to feel better; or even to be better? Do we think that positive thoughts can impact events, even when they appear out of our control? Or is there something more to our need to predict positive outcomes?

The answers to all these questions lie in the need to stop thinking of hope as holding belief that a desired outcome will occur. Rather, I believe we can unravel the contradictions and complexities of hope, if we think of it as an ongoing belief in the beauty of life's details, the opportunities for meaningful connection and the possibility of self-development; even when our situation is dire. As such, hope becomes a belief in our capacity to flow through all the seasons of our lives. A belief that we can experience both well-being and resilience as required, rather than determine any particular outcome. Simply put, if hope is about how we live, as opposed to what happens to us, we can embrace hope while still being authentic and honest during times of distress.

Most importantly, shifting our understanding of hope in this way means hope is no longer a means of avoiding negative emotions. Instead, hope becomes a vital element of living through the constantly changing seasons of our lives, with resilience. It is about self-efficacy and confidence, about accepting our authentic distress, supporting our wellbeing. It is about allowing us to accept impermanence and helping us to live with flexibility in all weathers.

If we can shift our understanding of hope, then being hopeful becomes akin to self-belief, even when our belief in a situation is wavering badly. Hope becomes something we can build, and which can build us, even when the outlook is bleak.

Rather than optimistically suggesting to others that 'everything will be OK'; let's help those struggling to reimagine hope as the belief that, no matter what happens, they can still find value in life. When life is tough, let's remind ourselves of our strength to survive, repair and thrive as contextually well people.

Let's understand and embrace hope as a way of living well; rather than a belief in always getting what we want.

TWENTY-FOUR

Trust in Life

THE ART OF RESILIENCE is about knowing how to heal yourself, and be a whole being in a constantly changing and impermanent world.

It is about creating a balance between being an individual and being a person, a social being.

It is about finding the balance between who you are and who you are constantly becoming. It is about creating and maintaining meaningful connections, inside and out.

When we develop the art of resilience, we become better able to nurture and repair our identity when it has been threatened or fractured. We understand the importance of acknowledging and accepting our reaction to trauma. We also value the power of supporting a congruent sense of our place in the world that aligns with our values. And we know to prioritise connecting with the world in a way that meets our core needs. Finally, we can move forward with trust in the possibilities of meaning and purpose within us and around us.

When I was studying for my PhD in Sheffield in the UK, I spent the last few months of my three and a half years there regularly visiting a psychoanalyst. In part because I am constantly interested in understanding the notion of self, and self-development; but also, to help me recover from the trauma I had experienced as a teenager.

Three Final Words

My therapist said little, as was his designated approach. The power of the sessions was in my opportunity to talk freely *to* someone, rather than *with* them. On reflection, I am not sure that the process was the best way to seek help but it was interesting. It allowed me to voice many hidden thoughts and fears, and to grieve the impact of events that I had never talked about. It allowed me the time and the space to go through my own bear hunt, and to begin to further develop the art of resilience for myself.

During my final session I asked my therapist if he could offer me any parting words of wisdom. I knew he was not there to advise me or to tell me what to do. Nonetheless it was the last session, so I pushed him.

He remained silent for what seemed like ages, despite my asking several times over. I nearly gave up waiting, wondering what all the sessions had been about. But then he cleared his throat, and said: 'Trust in life a little more.'

Trust in life. Was that it?

Three months of me talking and he had offered three words, six if you count the 'a little more' bit at the end of his sentence.

I wasn't quite sure what to do with this.

Ultimately, I guess because he had said practically nothing during three months of weekly visits, I decided that these final words had to be deeply significant.

So, I left that final session with those words indelibly printed on my mind. And since then, I have thought about them many times.

For years I considered that this quiet, thoughtful man was trying to simply suggest I worry less. To let me know that things would turn out better than I feared most of the time. I thought he was trying to encourage me to trust romantic relationships, which I had come to not trust at all. In this he was giving me a very good and powerful suggestion. Certainly, my lack of trust had led to my being glib or avoidant with romance a lot of the time. On other occasions I had become entangled in a new relationship in a ball of anxiety, through fear that it was going to go wrong. This of course was a sure-fire way of making it go wrong very quickly.

After leaving Sheffield, my learning to trust that things will be OK has certainly helped things to be OK more often – mainly due to my giving more things more of a chance.

In this sense, 'hope' can be compared to 'trust'. When we hold hope, we trust that life will turn out to be better than we might have imagined, or at least better than our current fears imagine it to be.

Yet, now I am so much older, and my life is so far removed from that time in Sheffield, I understand these powerful words in a slightly different way. Nowadays, I understand trusting life as learning to trust myself. As such, I am learning to trust the very core of who I am a little more every day. I am getting to know the unsocialised, uncultured centre of me.

I am learning to trust that 'I' am going to lead 'me' through life with my best interests at heart; because 'I' am 'me', at heart.

So, trusting in life still equates to believing that many situations will end up better than I believe they will, a lot of the time. But it also means trusting myself to the core. It means maintaining the belief that I can lead a life that feels authentic, and upholds my most important values, even when trauma and adversity occur.

In this, having hope really does mean trusting life.

Zen master Shunryu Suzuki Roshi suggested that we will make the biggest contribution to our world when we focus on creating connection and community in the immediate contexts of our lives, rather than trying to gain success with broader recognition, popularity or fame. With reference to the Buddhist Lotus Sutra, he said: "If you shine one corner [of the world], then people around you will feel better. You will always feel as if you are carrying an umbrella to protect people from heat or rain."

If we can learn to trust ourselves, while also embracing the impermanent beauty of our lives, everything really will be alright (mostly).

TWENTY-FIVE

Dance of the Pelicans

I HAVE WRITTEN THIS book in part while staying at my friend George's beach house in Western Australia. This was in February 2022, with the pandemic still headline news. I was undertaking a week of mandated quarantine having just returned from a visit to the UK to reunite with my extended family.

I had been frustrated at the thought of having to complete this week of solitude, yet, it proved to be a nurturing and incredibly creative time. It was, in fact, the first time I had had a week of looking after only myself since my first child was born nineteen years earlier. After the business of England, and the business of life, it felt like a luxurious opportunity to be wholly 'me'. I had time to meditate, to write, to watch what I wanted on Netflix, to do a bit of yoga, to eat when I chose… I had time and opportunity to do everything at a pace and in a way that was totally for me.

As I sat on the veranda during one sunny lunchtime, I drank a cup of coffee while watching the calm sea in the distance. The ocean is beautiful in this tiny corner of the world, as are the majestic Norfolk pines that framed my view. But the view was still and largely unmoving, and didn't hold my interest for long. I wanted to be able to simply enjoy the stillness around me, but in truth I was quickly bored.

Every so often a group of pelicans flew past. When this happened, I found myself immediately lifting my gaze, and following them as they danced through the sky. They moved gracefully, in perfect formation, with deliberation and grace. My interest was easily captured by the beauty of these prehistoric looking birds as they created moments of variation in the scene before me.

I realised that as much as I might fear the impermanence of many things; when I am listening to my inner voice, living by my values and taking care of myself; I am curious about, invested in, and brought more fully to life by the changes I experience in my life.

Life happens when everything changes.

So, how do we learn to live with change? How do we hold on to what matters, while also knowing how to let go?

If this is an impossible question to answer, is it a question we should even think to ask? Indeed, is there any sense in writing or reading an entire book about it?

I hope you agree, there certainly is.

The impossible question is impossible because it can never truly be resolved. It can certainly feel impossible to love something or someone and also be OK with losing them. Unwanted loss nearly always feels unfair, even when we know it is coming. It is hard to wholeheartedly embrace something that matters; perhaps even harder to let go. Yet, consideration of the impossible question is, in many ways, an answer in itself. Accepting the interdependence between connection and disconnection, growth and loss, joy and pain helps us to live our best life. Not 'best' in the sense of always being happy or enamoured with how things are going; but 'best' meaning 'fiercest' and 'fullest'. Considering the impossible question helps us to live with integrity, courage and purpose; embracing authentic connections and working through loss, never over it.

Moreover, exploring the impossible question of living well, frees us from a futile search for everlasting contentment, and the avoidance of pain. It helps us to find success in being more present, aware and invested in life. As such, the impossible question is the question we need to address, to help us feel our most alive.

As we explore the impossibility of holding something deeply to bring us a sense of completeness and joy, versus the pain of losing that connection and the inevitability of grief, we come to realise that we are dependent on change as much as we are lost to it. We begin to appreciate that a full and fierce life is not led in the pursuit of unending happiness; nor does it deny the inevitability of pain. Rather, leading a fierce life is about embracing our ever changing social identity within every present moment. It is about learning to be a person, flowing like glass.

When we build healthy authentic connections with an awareness of impermanence, we embrace greater self-determination and autonomy. We experience success as a life lived according to our values, even when our goals might fail. We learn to prioritise belonging and engagement, and know that these are the pillars of life's meaning.

When we learn to move through grief in all of its enormity, we learn to let go of resentment, and we learn to re-find ourselves at our core, however long that takes. We discover who we are under the many social layers that have defined us, and we open ourselves to the possibility of becoming authentically more.

It is easy to be happy when life is treating you well; and incredibly hard not to be sad when loss occurs. If we can learn to judge our life less by our contextual gains and losses, and more by our ability to dance with change; maybe we will find the true key to success.

ACKNOWLEDGEMENTS

The writing of this book has been a labour of love from start to finish. More so because of the incredible support of some very special people. First and foremost, thank you to Neil Porter. Neil helps me find the courage to take risks every day, feel the freedom to stay curious, and live with the confidence of knowing we are a true partnership.

Thanks also to my three daughters Lucia, Molly and Tess. I am a better person because of them, forever grateful to have them in my life. They keep me both grounded and flying high every day.

I wrote much of the first draft at the end of the Covid pandemic while undertaking a week of quarantine in Western Australia. Many thanks to dear friend George Burns who lent me his beachside cottage. My mandated week of solitude became an unexpected writing retreat. I will forever love the pelicans flying through the view.

I am hugely grateful to Selina Day. Selina provided me with reassuringly grounded and inspiringly intelligent editorial advice, along with some lovely conversations. Her belief in my work along with some very good suggestions added immense value to the final text.

Thankyou also for the earlier feedback and suggestions of editor Melissa Kirk. In particular, she helped me transform my many separate chapters into a cohesive arc, and for that I am very grateful.

And then to Sonya Murphy who once again has proved herself to be a consummate professional when it comes to formatting my text into a proof ready book – thankyou.

Oriah House! Another enormous thank you. I was beside myself with excitement when Oriah emailed me to give me her blessing to use her words to open the book. The Invitation is one of my all-time favourite poems. It is uplifting, inspiring and pretty much says everything I want to say in one exquisite burst of art.

Thanks also to my lovely friends and colleagues who kindly read the final manuscript and have written such supportive endorsements – John Marsden, Richard Ryan, Janis Coffey, Michael Carr-Gregg, John Hendry and Todd Kashdan.

The writing of the manuscript is only ever the beginning of the journey of a book. I would also like to acknowledge the wise and unbridled support of dear friend Sandra Devahasdin who has helped me share my writing with the world.

Thanks also to Troy Barbitta for the gorgeous cover design.

Finally, thank-you to you. Thank-you for taking an interest in this book and joining me on my quest to explore the impossible question of living well.

REFERENCES

and Further Reading for Interested People

The Invitation

'The Invitation' is taken, with kind permission, from Oriah, from
THE INVITATION by Oriah 'Mountain Dreamer' House
Published by HarperONE, San Francisco, 1999.

Chapter Three

Blanchflower, D. G. and A. J. Oswald, 'Well-being Over Time in
Britain and the USA', Journal of Public Economics, 88, 1359–86,
2004.

Boyce, C. J., G. D. A. Brown and S. C. Moore, 'Money and Happiness:
Rank of Income, Not Income, Affects Life Satisfaction,'
Psychological Science, 21, 471–5, 2010.

I wrote 'Standing without Shoes: Creating Happiness, Relieving
Depression, Enhancing Life' with George Burns following a lively
discussion about our shared views on the power of understanding
wellbeing as a means to preventing depression. The book was
published by Prentice Hall, a subsidiary of Penguin Australia, in
2003.

Philip Brickman's key publication that, despite contrary current research, is still widely cited today is: Brickman, P., D. Coates and R. Janoff-Bulman, 'Lottery Winners and Accident Victims: Is Happiness Relative?' Journal of Personality and Social Psychology, 36, 917–27, 1978.

Jonathan Gardner's more up-to-date and nuanced understanding of the relationship between wealth and wellbeing: Gardner, J. and A. J. Oswald, 'Money and Mental Well-being: A Longitudinal Study of Medium-Sized Lottery Wins', Journal of Health Economics, 26, 49–6, 2007.

Chapter Four

Sam Harris is a neuroscientist, philosopher and author. His excellent meditation app and associated teachings can be accessed via his website 'wakingup.com'.

Chapter Five

Hans Eysenck's personality inventory was designed to measure two major dimensions of personality, namely extraversion and neuroticism, according to the theory of personality propounded by Hans Jürgen Eysenck. It was published in 1963 as a commercial test by Hans and his wife Sybil.

Mindfulness teacher and author Jon Kabat-Zinn introduced this notion in his book: Wherever You Go There You Are, first published in 1994. In the book he suggests that 'wherever we go, we take ourselves with us', so we need to ensure we work on ourselves rather than on changing our environment, to feel happier.

Peterson, C., & Seligman, M. E. P. (2004). 'Character strengths and virtues: A handbook and classification'. New York: Oxford University Press and Washington, DC: American Psychological Association.

Chapter Six

This quote is from Professor Joseph Campbell's 1988 conversations with Bill Moyer: The Power of Myth. The popular television series was subsequently turned into a book: Campbell, Joseph, and Bill Moyers. The Power of Myth. New York: Anchor Books, 1988. 118–119.

Brené Brown states: 'Fitting in is about assessing a situation and becoming who you need to be to be accepted. Belonging, on the other hand, doesn't require us to change who we are; it requires us to be who we are.' In her best-selling book 'The Gifts of Imperfection' originally published in 2010 by Hazelden Publishing.

Chapter Eight

Professor Ellen Langer is one of the world's most influential social psychologists. Her work has increased awareness and understanding of the power of context in many settings including in our hospitals and in nature. Her Counterclockwise study is arguably her most famous work: Langer, Ellen (2009), 'Counterclockwise: Mindful Health and the Power of Possibility'. Ballantine Books: US

Contextual Wellbeing remains the book I most frequently talk to when working with educators. It has taken me to 15 countries to work in schools and present at conferences and events. Street, H (2018), 'Wellbeing – Creating Positive Schools from the Inside Out'. Wise Solutions: Australia.

Chapter Nine

Finding Mastery – conversations with Michael Gervais (podcast) 14 February 2018. Adventure Rock Climber Alex Honnold.

Free Solo (2018), Documentary directed by Jimmy Chin and Elizabeth Chai Vasarhelyi; Starring Alex Honnold, Tommy Caldwell and Jimmy Chin.

I have written several academic papers, articles and book chapters about goal setting, motivation and mental health. Three that are particularly relevant to this book are:

Street, H. (2001) Exploring the role of Conditional Goal Setting in depression. The Clinical Psychologist 6 (1) 16–23

Street, H. (2000) Exploring relationships between conditional goal setting, rumination and depression. Australian Journal of Psychology 52, 113

Street, H. (1999) Depression and the pursuit of happiness: An investigation into the relationship between goal setting, goal pursuit and vulnerability to depression. The Clinical Psychologist 4 (1) 18–25

Chapter Eleven

In the mid-1980s, Professors Edward Deci and Richard Ryan wrote a book titled 'Self-Determination and Intrinsic Motivation in Human Behavior' in which Self-Determination Theory (SDT) was formally introduced and established as a world-leading theory of motivation and self-actualisation. Since the 2000s, research exploring and expanding SDT has increased significantly, and the theory has also become a prominent theory of wellbeing. Two key references from 2000 are as follows:

Deci, E. L., & Ryan, R. M. (2000). The 'what' and 'why' of goal pursuits: Human needs and the self-determination of behavior. Psychological Inquiry, 11, 227–268

Ryan, R. M.; Deci, E. L. (2000). 'Self-determination theory and the facilitation of intrinsic motivation, social development, and well-being'. American Psychologist. 55(1): 68–78

Chapter Thirteen

Moss, Stephen (2012) Natural Childhood. National Trust: UK

Kellert, Stephen (2015) Build nature into education. Nature; London Vol. 523, Iss. 7560, (Jul 16, 2015): 288-289

Louv, R. (2005) Last Child in the Woods: Saving Our Children from Nature-Deficit Disorder, Algonquin Books, Chapel Hill

Moss, Stephen (2012) Natural Childhood. National Trust: UK

Sigman, A. (2007) Agricultural Literacy: Giving concrete children food for thought.

www.face-online.org.uk/resources/news/Agricultural%20Literacy.pdf

Chapter Fourteen

This research can be found in Mike Powers and Lorna Champion's paper 'Cognitive approaches to depression: A theoretical critique' published in the British Journal of Psychology, vol. 25, pages 201–212 in 1986.

Glynis Breakwell's inspiring book 'Coping with Threatened Identities' was first published in 1986 by Methuen and Co. in London.

'Noli illegitimi carborundum' – Pseudo-Latin. This saying was popularised by US General "Vinegar Joe" Stilwell during World War II. He is reputed to have learned it from British army intelligence. I have paraphrased the translation to be polite.

'A fool and his money are easily parted' – This long-established phrase is thought by some to have its origins in Proverbs 21:20 of the King James Version of the Bible. Others believe The proverb has been around since the 16th century and was academically first used in 1573 by Thomas Tussar in his famous work – Five Hundreth Pointes of Good Husbandrie.

'Laugh and the whole world laughs with you... cry and you cry alone' – The original quote 'Laugh and the world laughs with you; Weep, and you weep alone' is found in Ella Wheeler's poem 'Solitude' (1883)

'If it doesn't kill you, it makes you stronger' – Attributed to the
German philosopher, Friedrich Nietzsche who wrote: 'That
which does not kill us, makes us stronger'

'The art of living lies in a fine mingling of letting go and holding on' –
Written by Havelock Ellis in his 1973 publication: 'Affirmations',
Milford House Publishing Company

'We're Going on a Bear Hunt' is a popular and highly acclaimed
children's book written by Michael Rosen and illustrated by
Helen Oxenbury. The book was originally published in 1989 by
Walker Books, UK

Chapter Fifteen

Visit The Beck Institute of Cognitive Behaviour Therapy online at
https://beckinstitute.org/ to find out more about Aaron Beck
and his legacy. As the institute states: 'Aaron T. Beck, MD,
was globally recognized as the father of Cognitive Behavior
Therapy (CBT) and one of the world's leading researchers in
psychopathology. He was credited with shaping the face of
American psychiatry, and The American Psychologist has called
him "one of the five most influential psychotherapists of all time."
He was an Emeritus Professor of Psychiatry at the University of
Pennsylvania and served as Beck Institute's President Emeritus.'

Aaron's many publications include:

Beck, A. T. (1964). Thinking and depression: Theory and therapy.
Archives of General Psychiatry, 10(6), 561-571.

Beck, A. T. (1983). Treatment of depression. New York Times Book
Review, 88, 35.

Chapter Seventeen

To Shine One Corner of the World – Moments with Shunryu Suzuki.
Stories of a Zen expert told by his students edited by David
Chadwick, Broadway Books, New York, 2001

Chapter Eighteen

Professor Peter Gray's many references include: Gray, Peter (2011) The Decline of Play and the Rise of Psychopathology in Children and Adolescents. American Journal of Play. Spring, Vol. 3 Issue 4, p443-463

Flow is a concept described and explored in detail in Professor Mihaly Csikszentmihalyi in his book Flow: The Psychology of Optimal Experience published by Harper Collins in 1990.

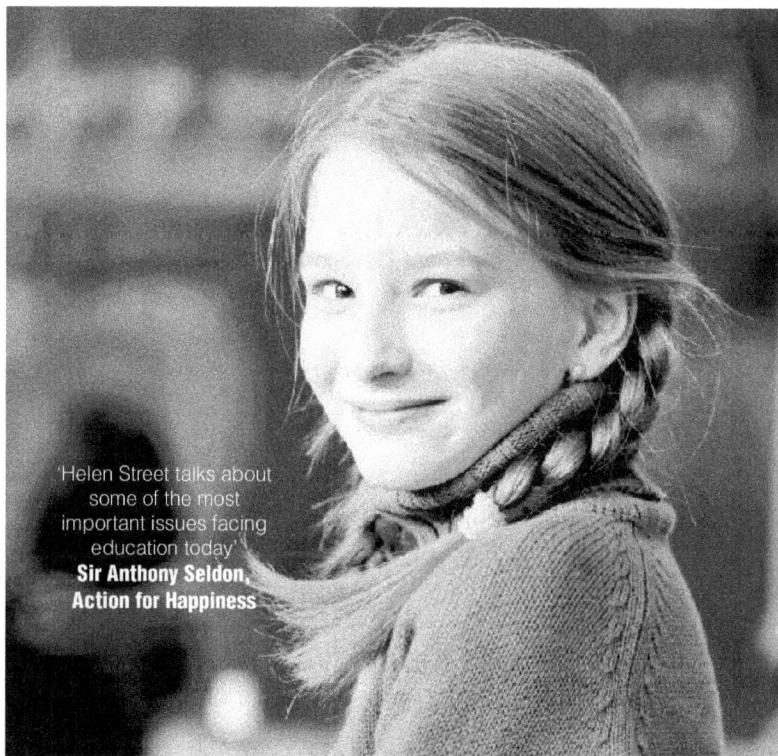

Are you a parent, educator or health professional who is interested in the wellbeing of children and young people?

Then Contextual Wellbeing may well be the book for you.

As an international best seller in education since 2018, this book has ignited wellbeing conversations, fueled contextual considerations and led to the genuine systemic development of forward-thinking schools around the world.

Available online from Amazon and all good book stores.

www.ingramcontent.com/pod-product-compliance
Lightning Source LLC
Chambersburg PA
CBHW060041030426
42334CB00019B/2431